Start T[

RIGHT!

Start Them Off RIGHT!

A Parent's Guide to Getting the Most Out of Preschool

Katarina Holtje

ALPHA

A Pearson Education Company

International Standard Book Number: 0-02-864326-7
Library of Congress Catalog Card Number: 2002106332

04   03   02   8   7   6   5   4   3   2   1

Interpretation of the printing code: The rightmost number of the first series of numbers is the
year of the book's printing; the rightmost number of the second series of numbers is the number
of the book's printing. For example, a printing code of 02-1 shows that the first printing occurred
in 2002.

Printed in the United States of America

Note: This publication contains the opinions and ideas of its author. It is intended to provide
helpful and informative material on the subject matter covered. It is sold with the understanding
that the author and publisher are not engaged in rendering professional services in the book. If
the reader requires personal assistance or advice, a competent professional should be consulted.

The author and publisher specifically disclaim any responsibility for any liability, loss, or risk, personal or otherwise, which is incurred as a consequence, directly or indirectly, of the use and appli-
cation of any of the contents of this book.

Trademarks: All terms mentioned in this book that are known to be or are suspected of being
trademarks or service marks have been appropriately capitalized. Alpha Books and Pearson
Education, Inc., cannot attest to the accuracy of this information. Use of a term in this book
should not be regarded as affecting the validity of any trademark or service mark.

For marketing and publicity, please call: 317-581-3722

The publisher offers discounts on this book when ordered in quantity for bulk purchases and special sales.

For sales within the United States, please contact: Corporate and Government Sales, 1-800-382-
3419 or corpsales@pearsontechgroup.com

Outside the United States, please contact: International Sales, 317-581-3793 or
international@pearsontechgroup.com

Contents

Book is mainly focused on preschoolers!

v

Introduction

Early childhood education is finally getting the recognition it deserves. Following thorough research, educators, psychologists, doctors, anthropologists, and scientists have reached the same conclusion: Early years are learning years.

We now know that a balance between environment and heredity, and nature and nurture has direct effects on the development of a young child's brain. What and how we teach our children will profoundly influence their learning abilities later in life.

We already know a great deal about children and their development, and we're learning more all the time about their minds and their potential. We also know that young children deserve the chance to learn, and we must be actively involved to make the right choices for them.

If you're a parent of a young child, these issues have probably touched you personally. You and millions of other Americans each year must face the decision of where and how to begin their children's education.

Instead of feeling guilty about going to work and not being present to personally introduce the world to your children and give them the fundamentals they need for basic reading, writing, mathematics, and social skills, you know the best solution is to enroll your child in preschool.

The sooner, the better.

And no, you don't want "baby-sitting," but a preschool where your child will truly learn and get the proper nurturing he or she needs. You want the best for your child.

Finding the right preschool for your child is a serious decision, but all too often it's made on an impulse, with little or no research beforehand. It's often based on someone else's recommendation that may have worked fine for their child but could prove totally wrong for yours.

It's a sad fact that many people put more effort into finding a new refrigerator than they do into finding the right place to begin their child's academic career—yet so much depends on your child's early years.

If you want to do it right, where do you begin? If you're a parent of a child younger than five, you probably have plenty of questions:

- Should you listen to the advice of friends or do your own research?
- What types of schools are best?
- What exactly is a Montessori school, and why does everyone talk about them?
- Should the school be near your job or near your home?
- How do you identify truly productive schools from mere "holding pens"?
- What's the right curriculum for your child?
- Should the environment be structured or laid-back?
- If you have a special needs child, will you be able to utilize a regular preschool?
- Will your child learn how to read?
- What exactly does accreditation mean?

Probably the most important question in the back of every anxious parent's mind is: Can you *really* trust your child with these people?

By now you've probably realized that only by doing careful research can you find the right match. Although your daily routine is likely filled with work, deadlines, rushed dinners, and perhaps an exhausting daily commute, at some point you'll need to answer these questions. Your child's adjustment to school later in life may be riding on the decisions you make today.

This book will help you take a step back, organize your thoughts, and begin the search for the best preschool for your child. We'll help you ask the right questions and look for the telltale signs of excellence in preschool programs.

For many, the term "child care" still does not go beyond its most basic meaning: taking care of children while parents are at work. This way of thinking perhaps was appropriate years ago when fewer women were in the workplace and baby-sitting and "low grade" kindergartens proved sufficient.

But the times and the rules have changed. Women today comprise a greater percentage of the workforce, and families often have no other choice than to enroll their children in some type of preschool. As a result, child care has expanded and can no longer be considered a separate service from education. It has redefined itself and grown into a new category: Early Childhood Education.

The fact that most of our children spend long hours away from home sobered many. The conclusion was simple and natural: Something had to be done about the quality of care our children were receiving. This improvement is progressing and there is still a lot to do, but we have come a long way in understanding the future impact of early child care on our society.

From whichever aspect you look at this issue, the conclusion is always the same: Today's children are tomorrow's citizens and workers.

As a result, enlightened employers realized much is at stake if employees don't have viable child-care options. Many have lost valuable workers because of lack of child care, poor quality of available child care, or simply because it was not affordable.

Creating a working environment nowadays without thinking of young families is not wise. Shorter working hours, opportunities for working at home, and better benefits are just some of the solutions employers choose to improve working conditions. Some have even gone a little further by providing child-care facilities onsite or have contributed to help defray the cost of child care. All this has helped parents balance work and personal lives, improved productivity, and benefited communities on many levels.

There have been lots of hits and misses as we learned what worked best for our children. Many layers of our diverse society made it that much more complex. Scientists, educators, social workers, policy makers, businesses, and, ultimately, parents realized that only together could they improve the lives of many children.

We know that children's development depends on how well they are nurtured. When educating a child, you must consider the "whole" child—their physical, social, emotional, and cognitive development.

This understanding has enabled us to advance our efforts to improve the quality of child care. All across the country, we started building preschools, adapting existing spaces, and training people interested in this field of study. Yet the demand for preschools is still greater than the quality currently provided.

Even though efforts were made to improve the quality of preschools on a national level, states and local governments are still setting inadequate quality standards. For instance, a close interaction between children and teachers in smaller groups is proven to have positive results in overall child development, yet child-teacher ratio regulations still vary widely from state to state.

We know that qualified staff, low teacher-student ratios, and age-appropriate education in preschools are tremendously important. The demand for qualified staff is great, but most often, these trained professionals aren't willing to work for the typical low wages.

On the other hand, if schools provide excellent facilities and the right environment for children, good working conditions, solid pay, and benefits for staff, many parents can't afford the bill. It's a conundrum seemingly without a solution.

Fortunately, many responsible, qualified, and dedicated people believe that every child deserves a chance and are out there making a difference. Their voices are being heard, and the effort to improve the present state of early childhood education is paying off.

Katarina Holtje

Acknowledgments

This book is a result of many efforts. Many thanks go to all involved in the project, especially to Carol Turkington, who helped arrange this book.

Thank you also goes to all my past and present colleagues with whom I have shared many rewards for patience, dedication, and vision. The magic land of inspiring children's faces was surely the best choice for all of us.

I am very lucky to have a wonderful family. My warmest thanks go to James and Mark for their immeasurable support. A very special thank you goes to Bert Holtje for believing in me.

Thank you to all my friends, of whom many are parents, for their encouragement. They, like many others, wish to give the best to their children.

Thank you to all who think that children count.

Chapter 1

Choosing a Preschool Program: What's Out There

We know how to find pearls in the shells of oysters, gold in the mountains and coal in the bowels of the earth, but we are unaware of the spiritual gems … that a child hides in himself when he enters this world to renew mankind.

—Maria Montessori

Karen, 33, was worried that she would never find the perfect preschool for the older of her two girls. "In my neighborhood I could have chosen from a Montessori program, a church-run class, or a program affiliated with the YWCA." But Karen agonized over her decision. "You really want to make the best choice—but it's not easy to figure out what that 'best' choice is."

Karen isn't alone. According to the U.S. Census Bureau, parents across the country are facing the same decision Karen did. In fact, the percentage of three- and four-year-olds attending some type of preschool program has increased from 16 percent in 1968 to 48 percent in 1998. That means there are lots of programs out there with sharply divergent styles, philosophies, and methods. Some obviously do a better job than others at offering a quality preschool education.

There are many types of preschools for parents to choose among, geared to just about every imaginable educational philosophy: schools focused on educational development above social development or social development before education, and others that mix the two. There are parochial schools and secular, public schools and private. Some, such as a Montessori or Waldorf school, follow a specific philosophical approach—but hundreds of others don't follow any particular philosophy. Instead, they mix and match various elements to create their own unique style of preschool program.

This book doesn't recommend one type of program over another—that's a personal choice. Only you know what's right for your children. What we can do is define the types of preschools available, help you understand what basic elements any good preschool should have, suggest ways to compare different preschools, and provide questions you should be asking teachers and administrators. There really isn't one single approach that could be considered the "best" way of implementing quality preschool education. It's a matter of your personal preference and the unique personality and makeup of your child.

Good preschools shouldn't have a problem answering questions about their philosophy and their teachers' qualifications. They should be proud of their school's philosophy and be eager to discuss it with you. (In fact, because most parents don't do their homework on early childhood education studies, good preschool administrators should be flattered you asked the question and interested in discussing it in depth. After all, everyone loves to talk about what they do for a living!)

Be wary of schools that either don't understand your questions or don't have straight answers. If they haven't thought it through and can't really articulate their philosophy, consider it a bad sign and don't put your child's earliest educational experiences at stake.

Basic Types of Preschools

If you're going to compare preschools, it's important to understand what types of programs exist in the United States today. Here's the rundown of what you can expect to find.

Public Preschools

Lots of different programs are included among publicly operated preschools, including those run by colleges and universities, states, or municipalities. Public preschools comprise the smallest percentage of the total number of schools in the United States.

For one Pennsylvania mother, a university-affiliated preschool was the logical choice for her family. "I wanted my daughter to go to preschool at a university because I figured the teachers would have the most up-to-date methods," explained Wanda, a high school teacher herself. "Most of the teachers were young and there were lots of students from the university who would come in to get teaching experience. I knew Catie would be surrounded by loving, caring people."

Nonprofit Preschools

Nonprofit preschools may be operated independently, or they may be sponsored by larger organizations such as hospitals or human service agencies.

Community organizations such as the YWCA often offer preschool programs. This is a choice favored by lawyers Barbara and Jim, parents of two children, who liked the fact that the program was located in an urban area with plenty of diversity. "There's not much diversity in our neighborhood," Barbara commented, "and we didn't want our children growing up with a distorted idea of their world."

Some towns also provide independent preschools that are not affiliated with any particular educational approach.

Many parents select church- or temple-run programs, which can vary widely in their philosophies and classroom activities. Some include lessons about the religion as a part of the daily routine, while others avoid most religious messages.

If you're considering a church-based program, visit the school and talk to the teachers so you can find out more about their approach. "I wanted a church-based preschool because values are important to me," commented Diane, 31. "But I didn't want a heavy-handed approach. I visited several church-run preschools before I found a place I felt comfortable with."

Religious Preschools

Along with building an educational and social foundation, parochial or religious-based preschools incorporate a religious element into their curriculum and teaching philosophy. When considering a religious school, you should evaluate how important religion is to your family and what role you want it to play in your child's education. The best place to explore options about religious preschools is at your place of worship. Remember that parochial schools charge tuition and possibly other fees.

For-Profit Preschools

For-profit schools are usually private, although a few may be sponsored by large national corporations. Good examples of private for-profit preschools include well-known chains such as KinderCare.

KinderCare is the leading private provider of early childhood care and education in the United States, both in terms of the number of centers it operates and the number of children it serves. KinderCare teachers are trained in early childhood development to provide lots of personalized attention and support, and centers are designed and equipped to meet the needs of all preschool children.

Founded in 1969, the company now operates more than 1,100 learning centers across the country. To meet the developmental needs of three- and four-year-olds, the schools offer separate programs for each age. Both are based on the latest research and best practices in child development and early education. Classrooms and playscapes are designed to encourage safe exploration, allowing children to discover, have fun, and learn.

The KinderCare philosophy centers on the idea that children do their most important learning before the age of five, which is why staff focuses on early childhood development. The schools emphasize age-appropriate environments that encourage children to learn, play, and explore.

Most important, at the heart of every project and activity is a well-trained teacher and an age-appropriate curriculum featuring hands-on experiences. The centers emphasize teachers who are warm, attentive, enthusiastic, and encouraging.

Preschool at KinderCare provides an enriched environment designed to foster each child's development, including discovery areas, outdoor playscapes, and a well-planned day with both small and large group activities. Lots of encouragement from teachers is an important part of the program.

When you visit a KinderCare preschool, you'll see that each room features clearly defined learning areas featuring lots of interesting materials and activities, including the following:

- Language/library areas: Areas filled with books and magazines.
- Math/manipulatives area: Areas you'll find lots of hands-on items that help children learn to count, group, and sort.
- Woodworking/creative arts area: Creative art activities are grouped in this area to help children explore.
- Home living/dramatic play area: Here preschoolers can dress up and enjoy role-playing and pretending games.
- Science area: Young scientists can use this learning area to explore basic concepts using materials like plants or animals.

Outdoor activities are just as important as learning areas in the Kinder-Care concept. Recess and outdoor activities are conducted in a playscape divided into separate areas to encourage learning through play. These various activities might include everything from typical playground basics such as sliding, climbing, and riding, to quiet learning, nature study, and imaginative play.

Every day, children in KinderCare preschools experience carefully structured focused group activities and individual play, small group interactions, and rest periods. The schools are careful to mix learning and play, quiet times and exciting moments, individual exploration and group activities. The KinderCare learning experts have carefully designed the curriculum so that it helps children master the skills they'll need later.

KinderCare features a literacy-based approach to literature to help children enjoy stories, books, letters, phonics, and early writing experiences. Daily activities support weekly themes so that children can develop a foundation in science, math, social skills, and creative activities such as music, art, and drama.

When it comes to reading readiness, KinderCare focuses on a comprehensive approach that includes phonics and letter recognition in addition to listening to books, poems, and songs. Basic math fundamentals are introduced with enjoyable math manipulatives to help children learn with a variety of informal learning activities. Teacher-led activities including grouping, sorting, counting, and ordering help children learn basic math fundamentals.

It's important not to forget that social skills are just as important as reading and writing, and KinderCare teachers help their students learn how to relate to others. Children participate in small and large group activities to get them ready to take part in social interactions, while imaginative play helps them practice the social roles that are an important part of society.

Occasional behavior problems are normal, but no child who misbehaves at KinderCare is ever embarrassed, ridiculed, or punished physically. Instead, teachers approach discipline with a positive attitude as a way of boosting a child's self-esteem. Tactics might include redirecting a misbehaving child to another, more appropriate activity.

Because a good working relationship with parents is essential for consistent, positive experiences in preschool, KinderCare teachers and administrators make it a priority to provide parents with details about what's happening in the classroom. Parents can expect to see daily schedules and weekly lesson plans posted on the bulletin board. Learning is extended to home through special weekly "learning at home" activities.

Teachers provide written assessments of each child's developmental progress at least twice per year.

Employer-Sponsored Preschools

Some fortunate parents can choose a preschool that operates right in the same building in which they work. Employer-sponsored preschools may choose to run their own programs, or they may hire organizations such as Bright Horizons or Childtime Learning Centers to run in-house programs.

Bright Horizons Family Solutions is a leader in employer-sponsored early education. Operating in the United States, Europe, and the Pacific Rim, the company has set up programs with more than 250 businesses, hospitals, and a variety of government offices. All of the child-care centers are designed to meet the standards of excellence set by the National Association for the Education of Young Children (NAEYC).

> The National Association for the Education of Young Children is the nation's largest and most influential professional organization dedicated to helping every child get the highest quality of care and education available. Founded in 1926, NAEYC has more than 100,000 members and a national network of 450 local, state, and regional affiliates working to improve early childhood education and to build public support for high-quality early childhood programs.
>
> NAEYC spearheads the effort to achieve healthy development and constructive education for all young children. NAEYC preschool accreditation continues to be one of the most reliable signs of quality care. The NAEYC website provides directories of accredited educational centers, along with guidelines for evaluating centers.

At Bright Horizons, the preschool learning environment is primarily based on the Creative Curriculum developed by Teaching Strategies, Inc.

The importance of the development of language, mathematical reasoning, and scientific thought is a primary philosophy throughout all the Bright Horizons.

The most important part of the creative curriculum are well-planned, separate learning centers that encourage self-directed play in small groups. At each learning center, a child can participate in guided experiences in a variety of skill areas, such as language, computers, science, dramatic play, outdoor learning, art, blocks, music, movement, sand and water play, and math manipulatives.

Throughout the day, children make self-directed and -guided choices using Bright Family "Choice Boards." They are encouraged to join in small groups and projects, participate in circle times with the group, and discuss what they've learned during the day.

Teachers design, adapt, and invent learning centers that best serve their students while following the Bright Horizons curriculum. The program is designed so that each child can learn all the necessary skills to succeed in kindergarten and to continue to thrive academically.

Childtime is another national provider of preschool services. For the past 30 years, the company has grown into a network of centers operating in 23 states, including at-work preschools operated in hospitals, corporations, government, and office parks. Currently, there are more than 30,000 children enrolled in Childtime centers nationwide.

At Childtime, children take part in an independently developed educational curriculum within a stimulating environment designed to boost self-esteem, self-confidence, self-help skills, and language abilities. Childtime teachers provide quality, developmentally appropriate programs for children in a safe, secure environment.

Childtime's curriculum focuses on the development of social skills, emotional health, thinking skills, and physical development. As the school year progresses, children become more independent and self-controlled by learning the right ways to take initiative while respecting others. Children are also encouraged to learn how to make decisions, reason, listen, explore their environment, and both articulate and understand their feelings. Teachers also help students improve their attention span by working on specific tasks for longer periods.

Childtime staffers encourage children to help each other, giving them words they can use to express how they feel and encouraging cooperation instead of competition.

At Childtime, children learn simple concepts and then build on these concepts so they are prepared to approach bigger and more complex tasks and ideas. For example, by using their senses, toddlers discover that objects have weight, volume, color, and texture.

Math concepts are another important part of the curriculum. By developing language and the ability to think in terms of classes, numbers, and relationships, children acquire the foundation for abstract skills such as reading, writing, and arithmetic. Childtime teachers help young children master these learning and problem-solving skills, expand logical thinking, participate in make-believe play, boost their speaking skills, and develop beginning reading and writing skills.

Childtime focuses on helping young children work on their gross and fine motor skills and use all their senses in learning. This can be achieved by making sure children have time for active play every day, using a variety of materials and equipment that require them to use their new motor skills.

The Childtime environment provides a safe space, equipment, and plenty of time for children to practice gross motor skills such as catching, throwing, skipping, climbing, and balancing. By mastering gross motor skills, children can then fine-tune their fine motor skills using muscle control and coordination. When children string beads, learn to zip, or line up shells, for example, they are honing their sense of direction, their eye-hand coordination, and their small muscle skills. Fine motor skills are important because they build a foundation for later thinking abilities needed for reading, writing, and math.

The federal government (including the military) is one of the largest providers of employer-supported early childhood programs. In fact, the U.S. military operates a vast child-care enterprise with more than 162,000 preschool-age children in 831 child-development centers. These programs tend to be of better quality because of the additional financial support they receive and the better benefits given to caregivers. These advantages often attract qualified staff, which automatically improves the quality of child care. In 1996, as part of the Military Child Care Act, Congress required that all military preschool programs become accredited. Currently, 95 percent of military child-development centers have met this requirement.

Public School Preschools

Although many states provide funding for preschool services, only a limited number of public schools provide early childhood education. Those that do primarily offer prekindergarten programs for children living in poverty or who are at some kind of risk that might interfere with their school achievements.

Head Start

The Head Start program is federally funded and operated by local community agencies, public schools, or other nonprofit organizations. This comprehensive program was created in 1965 to serve low-income families with preschool children.

The idea behind this well-planned program is to meet the needs of children and their families by providing good-quality early childhood education, health care, and social services for all children. An important part of the program is the opportunity it provides for parents to be actively involved in all phases of program planning, implementation, and evaluation.

Children from families meeting federal poverty guidelines are eligible for Head Start services. Programs throughout the country establish priorities for enrolling children based on community needs and available funds.

Ten percent of the enrollment opportunities in each program may be filled by children coming from families whose income is above federal poverty guidelines.

All Head Start programs must adhere to Program Performance Standards, and 93 percent of Head Start teachers either have degrees in early childhood education or are training for national or state credentials.

The Head Start Program Performance Standards are the mandatory regulations that agencies must implement in order to operate a Head Start program. The standards define the objectives and features of a quality Head Start program in concrete terms; they articulate a vision of service delivery to young children and families; and they provide a way to monitor and enforce quality standards. To locate a Head Start program in your area, search the Internet database of all programs at www2.acf.dhhs.gov/programs/hsb/grantees/search/search.asp.

Basic Must-Haves

Regardless of the type of preschool you choose, it should include as many of the following elements as possible:

- Meets the emotional, social, intellectual, and physical needs of each child in a safe and nurturing environment.
- Creates a stimulating classroom environment.
- Helps encourage a child's social development with peers and adults.
- Respects diversity, develops a sense of self, and promotes self-esteem.
- Helps children develop their thinking skills to the fullest.

Preschool Philosophies

In addition to deciding whether you're interested in a public or private preschool, you should also consider what type of philosophical outlook you're looking for in a preschool. Montessori, Waldorf, High/Scope, and Bank Street schools each focus on specific ideas about what they think is important in early childhood education.

In addition, hundreds of independent preschools around the country don't follow any one of the following approaches to the letter, but instead mix and match various elements of them to form their own program.

Montessori Schools

Sharon, a 42-year-old professional, was looking for a good preschool for her child, when a friend told her about a Montessori school a few blocks away. She had a vague sense that a Montessori school was "progressive" and required children to "be responsible"—but that's about all she knew.

Most Americans, like Sharon, have vague ideas about what a Montessori preschool is, but few parents have a solid idea of what's involved.

In fact, the Montessori method might once have been considered "progressive," but its theories have now been adopted by so many non-Montessori programs it's almost mainstream. The Montessori philosophy is based on the idea that a child learns best within a social environment that supports individual development. There are between 5,000 and 6,000 Montessori preschools in the United States, any of which may be private or public, for-profit, or nonprofit.

Maria Montessori

The Montessori method was developed by Italian physician Maria Montessori, who was born in Italy in 1870, the first woman to receive a medical degree in her country. After graduating from the University of Rome, she became interested in education as she began to treat children labeled "mentally retarded."

When she opened a care center for the children of desperately poor families in the San Lorenzo slums of Rome, she became so involved that she renounced all her academic positions and dedicated her life to the comprehensive study and education of young children. It was in this "Children's House" that she developed her program based on the idea that young children learn best in a nurturing environment, filled with develop-mentally appropriate materials that provide self-motivating, independent learning experiences.

Her theories included then-revolutionary beliefs such as the following:

- Children should be respected as individuals who are different from adults and from one another.

- Children learn through purposeful activity.
- The most important years for learning are from birth to age six.
- Children are unusually able to absorb and learn from people and materials in their environment.

Dr. Montessori's methods were based on her belief that children learn best by doing and not by passively listening and accepting someone else's knowledge and ideas. In other words, children learn best when allowed to touch, taste, smell, and explore their world.

She insisted on multi-age grouping—allowing children of different ages to learn together—firmly believing that older children are capable of "teaching" younger ones by influencing their behavior and guiding them in solving problems.

Montessori believed that all aspects of a child's growth—physical, emotional, social, and cognitive—are equally important.

At the beginning of the twentieth century, this innovative outlook on early learning interested educators, and her theories were widely accepted. Since then, many preschools around the world have adopted her approach.

It's hard to imagine a preschool in the United States that hasn't incorporated at least a few Montessori principles. Indeed, the Montessori method has profoundly influenced early childhood learning in preschools as we know it today.

The primary goal of a Montessori program is to help children reach their full potential in all areas, including social skills, emotional growth, physical coordination, and thinking abilities. The curriculum, under the direction of a specially trained teacher, allows the child to experience the joy of learning. Each Montessori preschool class operates on the principle of freedom within limits, with a set of ground rules that change from age to age, but that are always based on two core Montessori beliefs: respect for each other and for the environment.

If you visit a Montessori classroom, you'll probably find children freely moving around, working with carefully chosen materials on planned activities. You'll notice that children are free to work at their own pace with materials they have chosen, either alone or with others.

The teacher relies on her observations to determine which new activities and materials may be introduced to an individual child or to a small or large group. The aim is to encourage active, self-directed learning and to strike a balance of individual mastery and small-group collaboration within the whole class.

The multi-age grouping in each class provides a family-like setting where learning can take place naturally. More experienced children share what they have learned while reinforcing their own learning. Because this peer group learning is intrinsic to Montessori, you'll probably find more conversation in a Montessori classroom than in conventional early education settings.

Because Montessori preschools recognize that children learn and express themselves in individual ways, music, art, storytelling, movement, and drama are an important part of every Montessori program. You'll also find an emphasis on the sensory aspect of experience—What does it feel like? Smell like? Taste like?

A "True" Montessori Program

Because the "Montessori" name isn't trademarked, any individual or school can claim to be Montessori—and this is why you may find wide differences among preschools all claiming to be "Montessori" programs.

True Montessori schools are accredited by the American Montessori Society, which provides an added assurance that they adhere to the Montessori philosophy. In addition to accreditation and teaching credentials, the society offers regional workshops, symposia, seminars, and conferences to member schools. Schools accredited by the society must have the following basic characteristics:

🍎 Teachers: Teachers must be educated and credentialed in the Montessori philosophy and methodology for the age level they are teaching.

- Family partnership: The family is considered an integral part of the child's total development; you will be welcomed in a Montessori classroom.
- Age grouping: Montessori classes feature multi-age, multi-grade groups.
- The "whole child": You'll find a diverse set of Montessori materials, activities, and experiences designed to foster physical, intellectual, creative, social, and personal independence.
- Block schedules: Large blocks of time devoted to solving problems and seeing connections in knowledge.
- Atmosphere: Montessori teachers encourage social interaction for cooperative learning, peer teaching, and emotional development.
- Materials: A full complement of specially designed Montessori materials.
- An "open door" policy for visitors.
- Periodic visits from Montessori specialists.
- Adherence to the American Montessori Society Code of Professional Ethics.

The Montessori curriculum focuses on five areas:

1. Practical life: Children learn how to tie their shoes and put on their coats, prepare their own snacks and drinks, go to the bathroom without help, and clean up after themselves if they spill something.
2. Sensory awareness education: Exercises are designed to make sure children use all five senses to learn. For example, a child studying about fall gathers leaves and feels how brittle they are.
3. Language arts: Children are encouraged to express themselves verbally and are taught to trace and recognize letters as a precursor to learning reading, spelling, grammar, and handwriting skills.
4. Mathematics and geometry: Children are taught numbers through hands-on learning using concrete materials such as the golden beads that represent the hierarchy of the decimal system.

5. Cultural subjects: Children learn about other countries (geography), animals (zoology), time, history, music, movement, science, and art. All the disciplines are tied together in complementary ways.

Toys and other developmentally appropriate learning materials are laid out in the classroom so a child can see the choices and then select a task, called "work." Work options include books, puzzle games, art projects, and toys. When they are finished, children put their "work" back on the shelves and move on to something else. The daily schedule provides time for children to play alone or in groups.

Guides work with children individually and as a group, but most of the interaction is among the children. In a Montessori school, teachers aren't the only instructors. Older children often help younger ones master new skills. That's why each class usually includes children from a two- to three-year age span.

Montessori programs, based on self-directed, noncompetitive activities, help children develop good self-images and the confidence to face challenges and change with optimism. Children who require extremely rigid schedules may not thrive in the self-directed atmosphere, but most children do very well with Montessori. Special needs children, especially those with attention deficit disorder or other learning problems, often flourish in a Montessori program because of the individual attention they receive.

Montessori schools believe in teaching children about a wide range of cultures, and most actively seek a diverse student body. If you'd like your child to be exposed to kids from all walks of life, this might be the place.

Montessori-schooled children are often adaptable, because they have learned to work independently and in groups. Because they've been encouraged to make decisions from an early age, they tend to be problem-solvers who can make choices and manage their time well. Graduates of these preschools have also been encouraged to exchange ideas, to discuss their work freely with others, and to develop good communication skills.

Most Montessori schools take children starting at age three or four and prefer that they are able to go to the bathroom on their own. A typical Montessori preschool program runs from 9 A.M. to noon, and most offer afternoon or early evening care, too.

The Waldorf Approach

At the heart of the Waldorf philosophy is the belief that education is an artistic process, so every subject—even arithmetic or physics—must speak to the child's experience. A Waldorf program believes that to educate the whole child, the heart and will must be reached as well as the mind.

The basic tenets of a Waldorf education were established by Rudolf Steiner—an Austrian scientist, philosopher, artist, and educator. In 1919, Steiner founded a school for children at the Waldorf-Astoria cigarette factory in Stuttgart, developing the curriculum and training the teachers himself. By the time the school was temporarily closed by the German government during the 1930s, it had already gained international recognition and had inspired the establishment of similar schools throughout the world. In 1928, the first Waldorf school in North America was opened at the Rudolf Steiner School in New York City. Today, there are more than 800 Waldorf schools in the world.

Rudolf Steiner believed that children should be immersed in nurturing surroundings to stimulate and develop their spirit, soul, and body. This is why you won't find banks of computers or TVs in a Waldorf preschool; children are encouraged to engage in creative free play rather than watching TV and videos and playing computer games, because those activities get in the way of using all five senses to absorb and actively engage in life.

The uniqueness of the Waldorf system lies not so much in *what* the children are taught but in *how* and *when*. Waldorf teachers are cautious about introducing abstract intellectual concepts too soon, but instead emphasize guided creative play. The children in the Waldorf preschool learn in a gentle, dependable rhythm of drawing and painting, beeswax modeling, storytelling, and puppetry. The children also work at practical tasks such as baking, handwork, cleaning, and gardening. Preschoolers pretend they are chefs and actors, moms and dads, firefighters and queens. They sing, paint, and color, and through songs and poems they learn to enjoy language. They play together, hear stories, see puppet shows, bake bread, make soup, and build houses out of boxes, sheets, and boards. Waldorf teachers believe that to become fully engaged in such activities is the best way to prepare a child for life.

The preschool environment is simple, comfortable, and homelike, featuring toys made from natural materials like shells, stones, crystals, logs and branches, veils of rainbow-colored fabric, sheep's wool, wooden toys, and cloth dolls. While most preschools have arrangements in which different age groups are separated, multi-age grouping is very often the practice in Waldorf centers.

Waldorf schools believe that parents, caregivers, and preschool teachers have a responsibility to create an environment that is worthy of the child's imitation. The schools offer plenty of opportunity for meaningful and creative play. Waldorf proponents believe it's harmful to draw the child's energies away from these fundamental tasks to meet premature intellectual demands. Instead, Waldorf teachers try to encourage sound judgment, healthy vitality, practical intelligence, and an inner enthusiasm for learning.

A Waldorf preschool approaches all aspects of education in a unique and comprehensive way, following the different stages of child development. The curriculum is designed to address the emotional, aesthetic, and social needs of the whole child and to teach children to rely on their intelligence, their heart, and their hands. The schools try to nurture the emotions through the arts and by conveying knowledge with lots of hands-on experience. In fact, working with the hands in handwork and crafts, music, and the arts is an important part of the Waldorf experience.

Children educated in the Waldorf method are taught to have a creative and curious mind, a strong sense of morality, a love for meaningful work, a deep commitment to the tending of all living things, and a sense of joy for the evolving human spirit.

The name "Waldorf" is a trademark of the Association of Waldorf Schools of North America, so the Waldorf name can only be used to describe independent schools that have met the membership standards established by AWSNA. Only schools that have been accepted as sponsored or full members of AWSNA may represent themselves as Waldorf schools or use the words "Waldorf" or "Rudolf Steiner" in their names or subtitles.

Schools that are to be accredited as Waldorf schools must go through a series of stages of membership, beginning with "new initiatives." There are currently 27 new initiatives affiliated with AWSNA. New Initiative membership is for those interested groups that want to begin an independent Waldorf school, but have not yet begun their program. They must have a demonstrable commitment to the ideals and practices of the educational philosophy developed by Rudolf Steiner.

Developing school membership is the next step for those groups that have begun the implementation of a school program and wish to maintain and strengthen their ties with the mainstream of Waldorf Education through their ongoing relationship with AWSNA's regional committees. There are currently 53 developing Waldorf schools.

Prior to full membership, a school must be "sponsored" by a full-member school for at least three years, during which a member school advises the school it sponsors. Upon the sponsoring school's recommendation and approval of the school's comprehensive self-study evaluation, the sponsored school is admitted to full membership. There are currently 14 sponsored Waldorf schools.

Full membership indicates that a school has completed the preceding steps and can now take part in delegates' meetings to discuss concerns and act on association business. There are currently 48 full-member Waldorf schools.

Teachers are certified in the Waldorf method by taking a continuous sequential course of study lasting one to two years or during summer sequences.

Waldorf programs tend to be more group-oriented than those at Montessori schools. If your child thrives on order and rhythmic repetition, a Waldorf program may be your best option. But a Waldorf education can benefit almost any child, because Waldorf believes even children with special needs can bring something important to a group. (However, the program is not recommended for children with severe developmental disabilities.)

The Reggio Emilia Approach

The preschools in Reggio Emilia, Italy, have been described as among the best in the world, and their style has been distilled into a philosophy called "The Reggio Emilia approach." This whole-child system of early childhood education emphasizes art and the child's environment.

Although it has intrigued educators in the United States, there are very few true "Reggio-style" preschools here.

Still, it is easy to recognize what attracted early childhood education experts worldwide to the Reggio Emilia preschools. This affluent community in picturesque northern Italy has for more than 30 years been dedicating 12 percent of the total town budget to high-quality child care for children under 6 years of age. Today the community maintains more than 30 centers, which serve about half of the city's young children.

Their philosophy focuses on each child in relation with others—children, family, teachers, society, and environment—and activates and supports these reciprocal relationships. Classroom teachers listen to and observe the students closely, adjusting the curriculum accordingly. In addition, a teacher specially trained in the visual arts works with teachers and children to encourage expression through different media.

Reggio Emilia's approach reflects the way children are perceived in Italian culture—as a collective responsibility of the state whose upbringing deserves significant community support. The parental involvement in local government (through the school committee) concerning early age education and nurturing is vital. Parents are expected to take an active role in discussing school policies, child developmental concerns, and curriculum planning and evaluation.

This unique method is based on several basic and equally important aspects of early development:

- The look and feel of the environment in which children learn and socialize

- Long-term group projects initiated by children (including the process called the "Hundred Languages of Children"—symbolic ways of expressing ideas on the way to finding the right solutions)

- The teacher's role as an autonomous guide, observer, and facilitator of child-initiated ideas

The Environment

The look and feel of the classrooms in the Reggio Emilia preschools is crucial for learning. The rooms are connected by windows, passageways, and telephones, which encourages children to interact. Access to the community is assured by large windows overlooking the piazzas, and every classroom has exits to either courtyards or the nearby streets.

Walls, ceilings, floors, and entryways are covered with mirrors. Children's artwork, together with recorded conversations and discussions about current and ongoing projects, decorate the walls, posted on both child and adult eye level.

Classrooms are filled with plants, attractive and intriguing objects, and items that have been found by children on their outings. Projects are exhibited throughout the classrooms. There is plenty of space for supplies and materials, which are arranged in attractive ways.

Every classroom has large and small studio-atelier areas and clearly designated spaces for large and small group activities. There are small, intimate places for two to three children and larger common areas for dramatic play. The spaces are functional, easily accessible to children, and always aesthetically pleasing.

Teachers in Reggio Emilia often refer to their engaging and informative classrooms as their "Third Teachers."

Projects

The Reggio Emilia approach insists on integration of artistic expression as a tool for cognitive, linguistic, and social development. Projects can emerge from the children's ideas and interests and can be introduced by teachers, the community, and families. These ongoing projects employ all aspects of expression, including art forms such as drawing, sculpture, painting, print, music, puppetry, shadow play, and so on.

Multiple forms of representation, such as writing, counting, construction, and dramatic play, are considered to be the children's understanding of their experiences. This process of learning and emerging is called the "Hundred Languages of Children."

Children are strongly encouraged to explore all options on their way to solving problems. They negotiate while collaborating and discuss and evaluate their work.

As children communicate and face conflicts, solve problems, and revise their work, they are allowed to make mistakes and learn solutions. Another trademark of the Reggio Emilia approach is that children can begin a project without a clear sense of where it might lead or how it might end. This purposeful lack of structure, planning, and instruction challenges many internationally accepted teaching strategies.

Teachers work on projects with small groups of interested children while others choose from many other available activities. The projects are large enough to allow diversity of ideas, materials, and ways of expression.

The projects are based on in-depth studies of concepts derived from the group, and everyone's input is valued. The projects can last anywhere from one week to an entire school year—for as long the children are interested.

The Teachers

Reggio Emilia preschool teachers are learners themselves, and their autonomy lies in their lack of curriculum planning and achievement tests. They listen to the children, carefully observing and documenting their ideas and comments, from which they draw outlines for potential projects. They record every step of the project and use this information as a learning tool. They create individual and group progress portfolios by taking photos, recording videos, and writing down information. The teachers exchange their observations, portfolios, and experiences with other teachers, artists, and parents involved in curriculum evaluations.

The teacher's role is to explore with the children, provoke ideas, and help solve problems. They stimulate the children's thinking and collaboration with peers by exploring, researching, and learning together with them.

At the same time, teachers always foster the connections between home, school, and community.

The High/Scope Approach

High/Scope was established in 1970 by Dr. David P. Weikart, who started the organization as a way of continuing the research and program activities he originally began as an administrator with the Ypsilanti Public Schools. The name "High/Scope" refers to the organization's "high purposes and far-reaching mission."

This preschool program was originally created for at-risk urban children and was used successfully in conjunction with the government's Head Start program. Today, you're likely to find it in a variety of preschool settings.

The High/Scope approach is based on the theory that children need active involvement with people, materials, ideas, and events in an atmosphere of "shared control" in which adults and children learn together.

Although High/Scope preschool programs are compatible with the guidelines published by the National Association for the Education of Young Children (NAEYC), High/Scope is not a part of any regular NAEYC program.

High/Scope's preschool education approach is used throughout the world, and its research on preschool education has had an important impact on public policy and has contributed to the development of the Head Start program and other educational programs for young children. While High/Scope conducts research in a variety of areas, it is best known for its research on the lasting effects of preschool education and its preschool curriculum approach.

The High/Scope philosophy is supported by the Educational Research Foundation, an independent, nonprofit research, development, training, and public advocacy organization with headquarters in Ypsilanti, Michigan. The foundation was founded in 1970 to promote the learning and development of children worldwide from infancy through adolescence and to support and train educators and parents as they help children learn.

High/Scope foundation experts train preschool teachers and administrators, conduct research projects on the effectiveness of educational programs, develop curricula for preschool programs, and publish books, videos, curriculum materials, and assessment tools for educators and researchers. In addition, the foundation operates a demonstration preschool in Ypsilanti for local children and provides a model of "High/Scope in action" for visiting educators.

The High/Scope preschool approach is used in both public and private half- and full-day preschools, nursery schools, Head Start programs, child-care centers, home-based child-care programs, and programs for children with special needs. Originally designed for low-income, "at-risk" children, the High/Scope approach is now used for all kinds of children. It has been successfully implemented in both urban and rural settings in the United States and around the world.

The High/Scope educational approach for preschool includes a set of guiding principles for adults to follow as they work with children. These principles are intended as a basic guideline that teachers can tailor to the special needs and conditions of their group or community.

The primary philosophy of the High/Scope method is "Active learning"—the idea that children learn best by actively interacting with people, materials, events, and ideas, as opposed to direct teaching or exercises.

Children in a High/Scope classroom are encouraged to choose what materials and activities they would like to use. As the day progresses, children explore, ask and answer questions, solve problems, and interact with their friends and teachers. This kind of environment helps encourage children to participate in activities that foster developmentally important skills and abilities.

Although the High/Scope approach is newer than the Montessori approach, 30 years of research suggest that it can be effective in promoting children's development. High/Scope has identified 58 key experiences in child development for the preschool years and a wide range of practical strategies for promoting these key experiences. The key experiences are grouped into 10 categories. The 10 categories include the following:

- Imitation, recognition, role playing
- Talking, describing, scribbling, dictating stories
- Making choices, problem-solving, relationship-building
- Bending, running, dancing
- Singing, playing instruments
- Describing shapes, sorting, matching
- Arranging things in order
- Counting
- Filling, emptying
- Starting, stopping, sequencing

Unlike the Waldorf school, High/Scope includes computers as a regular part of the program; teachers select developmentally appropriate software.

The space and materials in a High/Scope setting are carefully chosen and arranged to enhance active learning. "Interest areas" (called learning centers in other preschools) are organized around specific kinds of play, with separate areas for blocks, art, playing house, small toys, computers, books, writing materials, and sand and water play. In each area materials are displayed so that children can get them out easily and put them away on their own.

High/Scope teachers help children develop a sense of control over the events of the day by planning a consistent routine that allows them to anticipate what happens next. This features the "plan-do-review sequence," in which children make a plan, carry it out, and then discuss their results. The daily routine also includes times for children to play in both small and large groups, together with time outside for recess.

High/Scope teachers are trained to participate as partners, not as supervisors or directors, in children's activities. High/Scope teachers focus on maintaining a positive interaction with children by sharing control, concentrating on children's strengths, forming honest relationships with children, supporting their play ideas, and adopting a problem-solving approach to social conflict.

Teachers use the High/Scope Child Observation Record for Ages $2^1/_2$–6 to evaluate children's developmental progress. Teaching teams take daily notes on a child's significant behavior during normal activities and then discuss the notes during daily team sessions. Later on, team members use their notes as the basis for completing developmental assessments at regular intervals.

High/Scope preschool teachers don't directly teach math, reading, writing, and other academic skills with activities, drills, or workbooks. Instead, they provide experiences and materials that help children develop broad language and logical abilities that build a foundation for later academic learning. For example, a child's beginning reading and writing skills might be encouraged by providing lots of books and materials, together with opportunities for children to listen to stories and work with writing tools and materials. To encourage math ability, teachers provide materials that help children use beginning skills in counting, comparing numbers, and one-to-one correspondence.

Children with special needs are not forgotten with the High/Scope approach. With these students, teachers emphasize the thinking, social, and physical abilities that are important for all children rather than focus on one child's deficits. In other words, they look at what a child can do, not what he can't accomplish. High/Scope teachers identify a child's developmental skills and then provide a rich range of experiences that would be appropriate for a normally developing child at that level.

Punishment and rewards are not used as tools for managing children's behavior. Instead, when behavior problems arise, the child is encouraged to discuss the problem as a way of developing social skills.

Art and music comprise an important part of High/Scope programs. Art and music materials are available for children to use freely at work time in most classrooms. Art is usually a small-group activity, whereas music is usually experienced in large groups.

The High/Scope approach is used in many Head Start centers, and many Head Start teachers, teacher-trainers, and administrators have been trained in the methods. High/Scope has also been a dedicated supporter of Head Start, often providing information and testimony advocating the continuation of the program. Nevertheless, despite this close relationship, High/Scope as an organization is not a part of the National Head Start program. High/Scope is similar to Montessori in that the basic philosophy is that children learn best by pursuing their personal goals and interests. In High/Scope, however, children are encouraged to make their own choices about materials and activities, and teachers are trained to support this independence and decision-making.

The High/Scope program is a good choice for any child who needs individual attention, including children with developmental delays and learning disabilities, because it's tailored to each child's individual level and pace. If you're interested in a very structured, adult-directed environment, High/Scope may not be the choice for you.

Whether a child needs to be toilet trained before starting is up to each facility. Some preschools are licensed to take children in diapers; others aren't.

Because of the urgent need for child care, preschool programs are expanding to include younger and younger children, and the High/Scope learning approach has been successfully used in settings serving children from infancy through kindergarten age.

The Bank Street Approach

The Bank Street preschool method was developed at the Bank Street College in New York City and features child-centered learning. The School for Children is an independent laboratory school for Bank Street College and a working model of the college's approach to learning and teaching.

The school is based on Bank Street's philosophy of progressive education and demonstrates the "ideal" representation of that philosophy in action. The preschool is the standard by which the college evaluates and improves education in other schools. The School for Children also serves as a benchmark of the kind of education that Bank Street is working to improve in other schools in New York City and school systems across the country.

Bank Street College of Education began as a research group in 1916, during a time when education usually consisted of a female teacher in front of the class lecturing or conducting drills. At Bank Street, educators were influenced by revolutionary educator John Dewey, who believed that a new and different approach to education could change society. He thought that children could become rational thinkers and contribute to a democratic society only if they were encouraged to inquire actively about experiences that related the outside world to the classroom. That attitude continued into the 1960s, when Bank Street faculty helped create Head Start and later was one of the major sponsors of Head Start's Follow Through program in elementary schools around the country.

Today, Bank Street emphasizes the education of the whole child—emotionally, physically, and intellectually. Bank Street teachers believe that in order for children to learn in school and to become lifelong learners, they must interact with their environment—so you'll find lots of hands-on experience here, including cooking, block-building, dramatic play, lab work, and painting.

Bank Street teachers emphasize carefully designed educational experiences involving talking, drawing, building, and acting. Children are encouraged to make discoveries from their observations, explorations, and experiences. Because students are directly involved with the environment and with learning, they feel more excited about learning.

Bank Street–trained teachers try to foster children's development by offering different opportunities for physical, emotional, cognitive, and social growth. These programs are based on the belief that children are active learners and experimenters but that they learn at different rates in different ways. Bank Street educators believe learning should encompass several subjects at once and occur in collaborative groups.

The curriculum is based on the idea that if children can learn about and study the human world, they can make sense of what they encounter.

At a Bank Street preschool program, you'll find lots of toys and materials that allow for imaginative play, such as blocks, water, art materials, clay, puzzles, and so on. Children can choose what they want to play with, and they can work by themselves and in groups. This helps them learn in their own way, at their own rate.

Like Montessori and High/Scope, the Bank Street program is less structured, leaving lots of discretion to individual teachers and children to decide what to work on and when.

If your child does well with an unstructured schedule, a Bank Street–based preschool would be a fine choice. The School for Children at Bank Street College in New York City accepts children starting at age three; other schools that use the Bank Street approach generally follow the same guidelines. If your child does better with more structure, you should search out an independent preschool that may adapt certain practices from these other schools but that provides a more rigid environment during the day.

Cooperative Preschool

If you just read through the entire list of available preschool programs, yet you can't seem to find the perfect school for your child, you can always join a parent-run cooperative preschool or start one of your own.

In cooperative schools, parents take turns volunteering as teachers and caregivers, and everybody decides what activities the children will pursue. If you've got plenty of time and energy, running a co-op nursery school can be very rewarding. For more information, visit the cooperative schools website at www.coopschools.com.

In the Next Chapter

Now that you've gotten an overview of the basic types of preschools that are available, in Chapter 2 we'll look at taking the next step—researching individual schools in your area.

Chapter 2

Spotting Quality: Preschool for Ages Two and Three

Although the term "preschooler" can include youngsters as young as two through age five, in fact there is an enormous difference in interests and abilities in that short age range. In this chapter, we'll discuss some specific things you should look for in a preschool program designed to teach children aged two and three.

Preschool for Toddlers

When you go to visit a preschool program for two- and three-year-olds, don't expect to find a silent place where all the toys are neatly stored on shelves and children are sitting at the table with their hands folded, chatting.

Children of this age learn through play experiences. What often appears to be "just playing" in actuality is a learning experience as children explore a variety of materials and participate in assorted activities.

In the real world, you'll find that most two-year-olds don't willingly sit still or at all. They move constantly, exploring. They have few social graces and aren't known for being quiet. This busy bunch is more likely to take all the toys off the shelves and leave them lying around rather than put them neatly away. Most of their experiences with art will focus on dipping their hands in paint and crumpling the paper.

Teachers

Preschool teachers for children this age must have many gifts. A good teacher will be able to wipe up spilled milk while giving a hug and reading a story—all at the same time. Teachers in this classroom must be magicians. Even the most carefully planned short trip to a nearby park can turn into an unpleasant event because of a temper tantrum. A good teacher is experienced enough to know how to shift gears and bring out a happy finger-play song (such as "The Itsy-Bitsy Spider") or a hug for the unhappy child.

Many have tried teaching this amazing age, but only patient teachers with smiling faces, soft voices, and big hugs have survived the ordeal. Even though the parent is always considered to be the primary hug-giver, it's healthy for children to establish close relationships with their teachers. Look for warmth, an engaging personality, and a sense of humor.

A good toddler teacher knows a lot about overall child development. This knowledge will shine through in a simple conversation with a child, and it will be obvious in the way the teacher corrects a child's behavior or greets you in the morning.

In a good preschool you're more likely to see teachers fully engaged with their young pupils. They should be on the floor, involved in and encouraging children's play. Teachers should be reading to individuals and small groups of children.

If a problem arises, you should see a teacher modeling interactions between the children. For example, a teacher will calmly but firmly intervene when one child wants another child's toy: "Sam, Jim is playing with the truck now. You can have it when he is finished. Now, let's go and get this airplane instead while you're waiting." Children this age can get easily frustrated because of a lack of words; hurting another child is often the fastest way to get a desired toy.

Even though it is good for children to learn to take turns and share, the best solution for this age group when such problems arise is to divert their attention. A good teacher will also provide multiple toys of the same kind and arrange the schedules and activities so children can learn to take turns while choosing what they want to do.

Watch closely for the interaction between children and teachers. Good teachers know when and how to respond to children and how to redirect them in a positive way. Most of these wonderful and patient people are truly gifted.

This age group is especially demanding, and the dynamics in this classroom can sometimes be beyond any adult's expectations. A child's attention span at this age is not very long, and keeping this group happy mainly depends on a teacher's resourcefulness and his or her ability to prevent accidents and incidents. Teachers in this classroom should not be afraid of a mess and should know very well how to deal with the unpredictable.

Pay attention to how many children each teacher must supervise. The ideal number should be no more than four children per teacher so that each child can get some individual attention.

Again, patience when working with young children is crucial. As much as repetition and persistence are the trademarks of children this age, much of the teaching in this classroom is based on the same principle.

Environment

The environment in a typical preschool classroom for two- and three-year-olds should be arranged to allow for plenty of moving around, free choice, the occasional mess, and lots of repetition—but still give the impression of predictability. Walls should be painted in pleasant and soft colors. Some primary colors, especially in small classrooms, can cause certain reactions in children. Strong red, yellow, or green or even busy wallpaper can cause restlessness and children can become overly active.

Sleeping, toileting, playing, and eating areas should be functionally divided. Sometimes a child will need a break from the group and require a quiet area to rest. These corners should be cozy, quiet, and covered with floor pillows and stuffed animals.

Young children spend a lot of time on the floor. Floors should be clean and free of clutter. Toddlers trip easily. The floor covering should be soft yet provide traction. Its colors and patterns should also be calm. Stronger colors and patterns may overstimulate children and make it hard to find a lost toy.

Look for diversity in the school's artwork on the walls. You should see pictures of children from different countries and of different racial and ethnic backgrounds, because you want your child to have the best introduction to the diverse world we live in. The pictures should always be posted at the child's eye level. Cheerful and colorful "real world" pictures are more likely to teach children than depictions of the latest cartoon character. Posters of violent characters from the latest children's cartoons and movies should never decorate preschool rooms. They may be scary to the little ones. It is every preschool's prerogative to provide real and positive experiences for children and prevent violence.

Check out the environment while the children eat. It's important to see how the meals are handled. Busy toddlers need careful supervision during mealtimes. It's not uncommon for youngsters to fall off chairs, choke on food, or just hold a plastic spoon the wrong way. An adult needs to be nearby to keep things on an even keel.

Lunches and snacks should always be prepared and set up in advance so that children don't have to wait. Meals should consist mainly of finger foods, because at this age children aren't very good at using utensils. Faced with spoons and forks, some children this age might feel intimidated and refuse to eat at all.

Social-Emotional Development

Social-emotional development at this age is in its early stages, and actions such as biting and hitting occur often. Preschoolers this age are becoming more aware of others and their own feelings, but they are often stubborn and may throw temper tantrums.

Preschoolers may still have trouble getting along with other children, and sharing may still be difficult. Because of their developing imaginations and rich fantasy lives, they may have trouble telling fantasy from reality, and they may also talk about imaginary friends.

Preschool toddlers need clear and simple rules so they know the boundaries of acceptable behavior. Teachers who understand basic concepts of growth and development for this age can help youngsters move through this stage.

Still, preschool toddlers also are developing a great interest in other children and enjoy being near them. By age three, children will begin to play cooperatively with other children in small groups, share toys, and develop friendships. They enjoy dramatic play with other children, but teachers understand children this age need clear and consistent rules and to know what the consequences are for breaking them. Teachers should encourage children of this age to express their feelings with words.

Because fears often develop during ages two and three—especially fears of new places and experiences—preschool can be challenging for children of this age. Teachers expect the preschool child to test them constantly, perhaps by using profanity or "bathroom" words and by acting very silly.

To help develop social skills such as taking turns and getting along with others, teachers will organize group activities such as singing songs in a group or building a Lego village.

In preschool, your child will learn how to separate from you, saying good-bye without too much fuss, and adjust to new situations (especially the school routine). Your child will be expected to learn how to trust and take direction from teachers.

Talking to children this age involves labeling and describing things and events—actions that help children develop their language skills. You should see teachers using simplified language so children understand the directions. Teachers should wait for a response from children and encourage them to speak. Children this age are learning how to express emotions simply but verbally ("I'm mad!" "I'm happy!").

Everything should be taken seriously here: holding a cup without spilling, successful toilet training, sharing, or just hearing "yes" instead of the standard "no."

Teachers should encourage a child's independence and allow time for practicing basic skills. By age 3, children should be able to dress themselves and button their clothes, stack 9 or 10 blocks, draw circles and squares, and use scissors. To boost independence and enthusiasm about learning, teachers will arrange activity areas throughout the classroom and encourage the children to follow their own interests and work on whatever projects appeal to them.

Children this age should begin to stand up for themselves when facing conflict. (For example, one child might ask another child to stop scribbling on her paper.) Good preschool teachers will encourage children to talk about their feelings and to resolve conflicts by using words instead of hitting or biting.

Children feel better about themselves if allowed to put on their socks or decide what they want to wear. They should be taught positive and accepting attitudes toward their bodies and its functions, and their readiness for toilet training should be respected. As a parent, you'll understand the importance of this.

Typical Activities

Preschool children this age are making rapid developmental strides and are deeply interested in the world around them. They want to touch, taste, smell, hear, and test things for themselves. Eager to learn, they profit best by being allowed to experience the world around them with hands-on activities. Play is the primary way toddlers learn how to use language and gain inner control.

Activities planned for this age should always be oriented toward process rather than product. In other words, the experience a child has engaging in an activity is more important than the result of the activity. Children should be given large watercolor markers, crayons, and large paper and allowed to safely explore. Food should never be used for art projects, because children at this age are still learning to tell the difference between food and inedible objects.

Preschools for this age group should feature lots of activities that enable children to explore: touching and tasting, music and dancing. Toddlers are naturally drawn to water and sand. Indoor/outdoor sand and water tables or boxes provide hours of fun for toddlers. They also teach many concepts such as floating, sinking, and weight. Soft toys are also very popular; stuffed animals, cushions, and blankets are some favorites.

There should be a dress-up corner with at least a box of hats and a mirror. "Pretending" is the best way of learning and is also one of every toddler's favorite activities.

Physical Activity

Even though children this age don't need to be reminded to be active, the preschool should encourage appropriate physical activities. Although all preschoolers reach various developmental stages at different times, by the age of three children should be able to walk up the stairs with alternating feet, jump, hop, walk on toes, pedal a tricycle, stand on one foot, build towers of six to nine blocks, and catch a ball.

They should be able to smear or dab paint and draw in vertical, horizontal, and circular motions and handle small objects such as puzzles or pegboards.

Children this age need to try out different ways to move their bodies. They should be doing things in the community such as taking walks and visiting libraries, museums, informal restaurants, parks, beaches, and zoos.

Activities necessary for promoting physical development change as each child gets older. For example, young preschoolers at about age three can be expected to have more advanced gross motor skills (which involve the large muscles of the body) when compared to fine motor skills (control of the fingers and hands). For this reason, different kinds of activities and equipment are needed for a three-year-old than what would be appropriate for a five-year-old.

The youngest preschool children usually need activities that provide a chance to develop and refine fine and gross motor skills, improve balance and coordination, and increase strength.

Books

There should be plenty of sturdy books with easy-to-turn pages. Take the time to pick up a book or two off the shelves and review the contents: the fewer commercial characters, the better. There is nothing wrong with an occasional friendly Winnie the Pooh book, but seeing books featuring pictures of nature and animals or books about shapes, colors, and the alphabet is a much better sign. Nothing substitutes for a picture of a real and friendly face or a familiar object.

Many schools have their own books or regularly go to local libraries, but some schools have amassed their book collections primarily from donations. People tend to get rid of outdated, damaged, dirty, or commercial children's books by giving them to preschools. This is why it's important to check out the quality of the school's offerings.

Toys

Blocks should be large and light enough to carry and stack and made out of both wood and plastic so children can experience different textures, weight, and shapes. Puzzle pieces should have small knobs for easy handling and usually consist of no more than 10 pieces. Toys in general should be easy to manipulate, without small removable parts that can be swallowed. Remember, children this young are still prone to exploring their surroundings by mouth.

Check to see if the toys in the classroom have features that will intrigue a two-year-old: A telephone dial or an old computer keyboard are excellent interactive toys that will provide entertainment for a long time.

Television and Movies

Although there's nothing inherently bad about TVs and videos at home, having these in a toddler classroom can be a bad sign. Passive TV viewing is not what you are paying for in a good preschool, because it's not stimulating your child's creative energies. Children in front of a TV are *watching*, not *doing*—and "doing" is important at this age.

If movies *are* part of the curriculum, viewing time should be limited to about one half-hour, given the short attention span of children this age, and only once a week. The content should be of good quality, noncommercial, and educational. Music videos and videos focusing on language skills are good choices.

Guidelines for Age Two: High-Quality and Low-Quality Programs

As you prepare to visit preschools for your child aged two or three, there are certain things you're going to want to watch for that illustrate a good program—and some things you don't want to see. Following are some guidelines that will help you know what to look out for, with details about both good and poor preschool programs for two-year-olds.

Teacher Qualifications

High-Quality Program

Teachers have at least an Early Childhood Teaching certificate, some experience in working with toddlers and three-year-olds, and up-to-date CPR and successfully completed first-aid training. This training is particularly important, because children this age are more prone to choking. Teachers also need to be in good health and regularly go through medical examinations. Anyone who works with children should be free of any communicable diseases.

Low-Quality Program

Teachers do not have experience, have very little training, and are not trained in first aid and CPR. They haven't passed their required medical examination.

Teacher-Child Interaction

High-Quality Program

In a good program, teachers will get down on the child's level, letting the child begin the conversation and respecting the child's lead. Teachers won't speak for or answer for the child, but will wait for the child's response—even from children who have limited language skills.

In an effort to teach children new words, teachers will label objects and reflect feelings and describe events in simple language for youngsters just learning to express themselves. You'll hear good teachers "expand" on a child's sentences. If a two-year-old says, "Harry's book!" the teacher might respond, "Oh, I see you've found Harry's book. He left it on the stool."

Many toddlers this age have a favorite object they like to take everywhere they go. Bringing these objects to school helps children feel more secure. There's absolutely nothing wrong with these so-called transitional objects, and good teachers will respect a child's preferences. They understand that having strong preferences for familiar objects, food, or people is a good sign of a developing sense of self. Teachers should allow children to carry their teddies and blankets and give them the chance to gradually lose this dependence as they help them get used to the new environment.

In a good program, teachers watch what a child is trying to do and provide encouragement but don't immediately jump in and take over. They will, however, be willing to help with a task if the child is getting frustrated.

You would expect to see a good teacher respond immediately if a child is crying or asking for help, because children this age don't have extensive language ability.

Disputes between children—for example, over a toy—are inevitable in even the best programs. When problems erupt, a good teacher will intervene and either provide a similar toy for both children or remove the disputed toy. Children who are edging out of control will be redirected in an attempt to help them control their own behavior. For example, if Suzy begins to lose control when she can't play with Sarah's doll, a good teacher will pick up an interesting picture book and try to interest Suzy in looking at pictures instead. This type of distraction is often enough to interrupt the developing tantrum. If the child continues to spiral out of control, a good teacher will simply remove the child to another play area. Change of environment and pace often work well, but not immediately.

Tantrums can be pretty severe, and the teacher must ensure that both upset child and surrounding children are safe. Kicking and screaming are usual, but in some cases children are capable of seriously hurting themselves and others. Tantrums should never be ignored. Teachers can, if they see it to be the only option, restrain the child physically by holding their arms or feet, but only mildly and only for the purpose of preventing self-inflicted injury or injuries to others. The best teachers remain calm and patient during the "storm" and make sure that a tantruming child eventually starts responding to words.

Toddlers might resort to purposeful "bad behavior" to get attention. In this case, teachers should definitely let them know about the limits. Again, if teachers set firm rules about hitting, biting, kicking, and so on, children will feel more secure. Limits, as long as they are appropriate and reasonable, will help children cope with the overwhelming world they are only beginning to learn about.

Children should be taught to be responsible for their behavior. Toddlers are only responding to their primal urges; the nervous system and language are still in the earlier stages of development. It is hard for children to understand the principles of social interaction. Being consistent in letting them know what is inappropriate is always best. Social development is usually the last perfected area in any child's life.

One thing you can expect to hear among children this age is an emphatic "No." Good teachers aren't upset or surprised by this, but recognize that negative behavior is a hallmark of two-year-olds. Con-stantly testing limits is just a way for children this age to develop a sense of themselves as separate human beings. At the same time, when issuing directions to children, good teachers aim for positive direction: "Here, you can punch this pillow" instead of "Don't punch the wall." "No" from a teacher should be reserved for actions that affect a child's safety.

There should be lots of modeling behavior going on in a good classroom as teachers show toddlers the right way to handle frustrating situations. Many times children this age resort to negative behavior because they lack vocabulary and simply don't know any other way to deal with a situation, such as sharing a toy. A good teacher will model for the child how to handle this situation: "Jerome, I want the ball now."

When you walk in the door you'll know a good program right away by the warm, friendly greeting from staff. Transitions are often difficult for this age group, so teachers make a point of settling the child into the daily routine by helping them find a book or begin quietly playing with another child.

In a good program, teachers give appropriate praise when children accomplish something, complete a task, or handle an interpersonal situation well. This helps the child develop a sense of competence.

Low-Quality Program

What you don't want to see in a classroom is a teacher who either dominates the class, talking at children without waiting for a response, or who ignores students altogether because she assumes they're too little to answer. Also watch out for language extremes: either teachers who use baby talk with two-year-olds or who speak in far too complex ways for young toddlers.

In a less-than-desirable classroom, teachers interfere with a child's favored personal objects, snatching them away from children or requiring them to share them with other children. Children are not allowed to make choices. In poor classrooms, all children are expected to do the same thing, and their preferences are ignored. Socializing among children is minimal because children are not allowed to gather in small groups and interact. In a low-quality classroom, teachers expect either too much or too little of children, leaping in and taking over when a child is trying to do something because it's faster for the teacher to do it herself. At the other end of the spectrum, you don't want to see a teacher who allows a child to become frustrated when trying to do something beyond his capability.

Teachers in a low-quality class will ignore a child's tears or respond inconsistently. If arguments erupt, the teachers ignore the fights or overreact and punish any infraction severely. Shaming children is commonly used as a way to punish in this type of program.

In a low-quality classroom, teachers punish an aggressive child inappropriately, which only worsens the situation. They may lose their temper, shout at a child, or reveal a lack of patience under stress.

Less-than-ideal programs don't have a good way to begin the day. The teachers don't make a point of greeting the children, and children are expected to help themselves to a book or toy right away without any teacher contact.

In a poor preschool, you may find teachers criticizing toddlers for not being able to do something or shaming them for their inability to master a task. Equally problematic is a teacher who overprotects a child and makes the child feel inadequate.

Curriculum Issues

High-Quality Program

Teachers in a good program recognize that participation is a vital part of any preschool program, even for two-year-olds. They read to children alone or in groups of two or three, act out simple fairy tales with the children taking all the parts, and let the children manipulate figures on a flannel board. There is lots of singing and finger play for everybody to participate in.

In a good art class, children are given all sorts of materials such as large sheets of paper and large watercolor markers or crayons that the children can use as they wish. A good teacher wouldn't set up a still life for children this age and expect everyone to produce a good likeness—in fact, good teachers don't expect children this age to produce a finished product at all. Teachers would never give children a big bowl of uncooked macaroni and ask them to make art pictures with it, because children this age are still learning how to tell the difference between food and nonfood objects.

Playtime is extremely important developmental work for two-year-olds, and good teachers understand how vital this is. Children are allowed to play alone, in parallel, or in groups, as they wish. As a way of maintaining harmony, the program provides duplicates of the most popular toys.

Toilet training in a good preschool is based on positive reinforcement. Children are invited to use the toilet and are provided whatever help they need. They are taken to the toilet often (which is located in a pleasant, private place), and they are never shamed or scolded for having an accident.

Because good preschools recognize the importance of outdoor exercise, they offer daily opportunities for exploration whenever the weather allows. Both water and sand play is available outdoors.

The nutritional needs of two-year-olds are different than for older children, and good preschools recognize this. You can expect to find snacks such as graham crackers, pretzels, fruit, or yogurt offered more often and in smaller portions than for older youngsters, with plenty of drinks available. Milk, fruit juice, and water are standard good choices. Soda is not acceptable. Teachers serve lots of finger foods, and if utensils and cups are used they are toddler-friendly, such as child-size spoons or "sippy cups."

Many younger toddlers are still attached to baby bottles and pacifiers. Teachers can cooperate with parents to discourage this habit by limiting their use. Baby bottles and pacifiers can affect the development of teeth, speech, and social skills. For instance, if a child's pacifier is in his mouth all the time, chances are that his speech will not develop properly, which decreases his chances of interacting positively with others.

You'll find a predictable regularity to the schedule in a well-run preschool program, but there is still enough flexibility to make changes if that's in the best interests of the children. Still, the general day-to-day rhythm is familiar, which makes children feel secure.

In a good preschool, teachers see routines as ways for children to become more independent.

Low-Quality Program

In a poor program, you'll find teachers grouping large numbers of children together, forcing them to passively watch an activity. Children are not encouraged to take part themselves, but must remain a quiet "audience."

Too much help is given by teachers in a poor preschool as children dabble in art. Teachers provide a model of what an object "should" look like and require children to make this model. Other inappropriate practices include handing out mimeographed pages from a coloring book that children are then required to fill in.

Inappropriate preschool programs do not understand the importance of play or value play for play's sake, or try to force all the children to play together instead of allowing them to engage in solitary or parallel play. These programs don't bother to provide duplicates of popular toys, so constant fights break out over who gets the toy next.

A rigid approach to toilet training is inappropriate. In poor preschools, children are forced to sit on the toilet whether they are developmentally ready or not (and certainly not all two-year-olds are ready). They are made to sit on the toilet for long periods and are punished or shamed for having accidents.

Because water and sand play can be messy and require supervision, less-than-optimum programs don't offer these opportunities. Teachers explain they don't allow this play because children eat sand or get wet.

In a low-quality program, food is used as a reward, doled out on the adult's schedule without regard for a young child's nutritional needs. Food is too often served only on a rigid schedule, so that even if young children begin to get fussy, a snack will not be served early.

Schedules in a low-quality program are either unfailingly rigid and based on adults' needs or are nonexistent, so children have no sense of consistency.

Learning tends to foster a feeling of dependence in a low-quality program. Teachers too often complete routine tasks, such as putting on shoes and dressing or helping with utensils. Utensils are not chosen specifically for ease of use.

Environment

High-Quality Program

When you walk into a top-notch preschool, you'll notice that the environment is set up with two-year-olds in mind. You should see separate areas for eating, sleeping, and playing, with both hard elements such as rocking chairs, and soft items such as pillows, carpeting, and thick rugs. There are little cubbyholes with private areas for no more than two children at a time, and the decoration is cheerful and friendly. Art is positioned at a child's eye level.

Children will have their own beds and bedding and their own utensils and special comfort objects, and their names are used to label personal items.

Exercise is important, and good preschools offer safe, appropriate play equipment outdoors so children can safely stretch their muscles. The outdoor play space should be separate from playgrounds for older children, and include small climbing equipment, low slides, and swings. Supervision is always available.

Good teachers make sure that toys are displayed on accessible shelves and that children can retrieve them on their own. Children are also allowed to carry the toys from one area to the next with relative freedom.

Low-Quality Program

In a low-quality program, you'll see mostly hard surfaces because they're easier to keep clean. The school is dark and depressing, perhaps not as clean as it should be, and decorations are hung at adult level. There are no private places for children to hide away and sleeping-eating-playing areas are all open and too noisy.

In a low-quality program, children take naps in shifts, sharing beds. They don't have their own supplies, and personal items from home are forbidden.

Watch out for a program that doesn't offer plenty of equipment for exercise. Poor programs either don't have outdoor play areas or offer equipment that's too big and unsafe for two-year-olds. Indoor space is too dark and cramped to allow youngsters to really be able to exercise freely. Toddlers share outdoor space with older children, and teachers are often distracted or unavailable for direct supervision.

In a low-quality program, toys are dumped helter-skelter in a huge toy box or locked away on high shelves to be doled out by teachers.

Health and Safety

High-Quality Program

Good hand-washing hygiene is imperative in a program with toddlers, and you'll find that teachers in these schools are diligent about washing their hands before and after each diaper change, before and after helping a child on the toilet, and before handling food.

The spread of infection in a preschool with two-year-olds is a constant concern. In a good preschool, teachers are careful to wash toys with a bleach solution after a child has been mouthing them. Toys are also washed each night. Diaper-changing tables are sanitized after each change.

Check around the building; a good preschool will have taken care of all obvious safety issues. Outlets are covered, extension cords and blind cords are kept out of reach, and hazardous substances are locked away.

Low-Quality Program

In a program where health and safety aren't paramount, you may see teachers be far too casual about washing their hands after diapering, preparing snacks, wiping noses, and so on.

Toys are scattered all over the floor and are seldom cleaned. If they are cleaned, the teachers don't use a bleach solution, but simply run them under cold water. Teachers don't hesitate to change several children's diapers on the same surface without sanitizing in between.

In a low-quality program, teachers have so many children in their charge they can't detect changes in normal patterns of behavior—and miss indications of illness.

Children are too often simply told not to touch dangling cords or outlets in a low-quality program.

Parent-Teacher Interactions

High-Quality Program

You can always recognize a preschool with good parent-teacher relations when your status as parent is respected and supported. In a good preschool, teachers respect your opinion as the person who knows your child best.

On your first visit with your child, the teacher should greet you both warmly. Cheerful and optimistic staff should readily communicate pertinent information about the day's activities, and after listening to you carefully, they should reassure you that any concerns you might have deserve attention.

You can recognize a good preschool by the quality of its staff: Teachers enjoy working with two-year-olds and are warmly affectionate and patient. They have a degree in early childhood education and have had training in the two-year-old age group.

Good programs allow no more than 6 toddlers for any 1 teacher (and fewer children per adult is better); the maximum overall group size is limited to 12.

If you see teachers chatting with parents on a daily basis, you know you've got a good preschool. Good teachers keep detailed daily records they are willing to share with parents, in addition to formal biannual conferences.

Low-Quality Program

Teachers who treat parents as ignorant nuisances are typical of inappropriate preschool programs. In such a school, you'll find an attitude of "we know what's best for your child; *you're* just the parent." In these programs, teachers may not bother to greet parents at all or are abrupt and unfriendly in their interactions.

The sense you might get in a low-quality program is that teachers have been "stuck" with the two-year-old group, that this type of work is difficult, and that they take a custodial approach to the job. Teachers like this either push toddlers too much and expect too much of them, or they don't expect enough. They likely have no training or experience in early childhood education and have little idea what constitutes appropriate behavior in a two-year-old.

If the staff-child ratio is more than six to eight toddlers per one teacher, you're looking at a low-quality program, where close super-vision and individual attention are almost impossible. Emphasis is placed on controlling the group instead of responding to individual needs.

Teachers rarely bother to share information about children with parents in a low-quality program, getting together only during planned conferences. No daily schedules or weekly summaries of a child's behavior are ever prepared.

Guidelines for Age Three: High-Quality and Low-Quality Programs

Now let's look at some guidelines for spotting quality preschools for your three-year-old.

Teacher Qualifications
High-Quality Program
Much like toddler teachers, teachers of three-year-olds have proper training in first aid and CPR and are in good health. They have degrees in early childhood education or a related field. Many good programs require at least a Bachelor's degree, and it is not rare to see that lead teachers and program coordinators have a Master's degree.

Low-Quality Program
Teachers do not have degrees in the field or such, and in some instances their formal training in child development and health and safety has not been completed.

Teacher-Child Interaction
High-Quality Program
In a good preschool, teachers realize that three-year-olds are different from two-year-olds. At this age, youngsters are usually far more cooperative and want to please—but teachers also understand that occasional reversion to "terrible two" behavior in new situations is not unusual. They also realize that to a three-year-old, independence is very important. Teachers in a good school allow children this age to perform as many tasks as possible on their own, stepping in to help only when needed.

Because they realize how important independence is, these good teachers provide lots of opportunities for three-year-olds to feed themselves, help set and clear the table, dress and undress, wash hands, and pick up toys.

Good teachers know that three-year-olds aren't always the best eaters, and that it's perfectly normal for them to refuse some foods or eat only a little.

Good teachers always respond to three-year-olds clearly and warmly, listening to their answers and patiently answering their questions. They understand that for children this age, talking may be more important than listening and understand that three-year-olds often ask questions they already know the answers to just so they can practice giving the answers again and again. Good teachers understand that acquiring language is important business for children this age and are endlessly patient in conversation.

Low-Quality Program

In a less-than-perfect preschool, teachers may tease or scold three-year-olds when they behave like toddlers, expecting too much of them. They aren't willing to allow an occasional "regression" during times of stress or in a new situation.

Teachers in low-quality programs expect far too much of a three-year-old, either hurrying them along and doing tasks these children could do on their own, or leaving them to their own devices for long periods of time.

They too often step in and take over routine chores (such as setting the table or wiping up afterward) because it's faster and easier than having children do it, or they insist that children pick up all the toys by themselves, all the time. You'll find some teachers who scold or shame a child who has an accident.

In a low-quality program, teachers have preconceived ideas of how much children should be eating. Youngsters are punished or pressured into eating the large meals that are served, regardless of whether or not they're hungry.

Discipline in a low-quality classroom is strict, as teachers try to keep everyone quiet—and punish those who talk a lot. Teachers in general speak only to the whole group, rarely to an individual child except to discipline one. Teachers get exasperated or ridicule children who ask too many questions.

Curriculum Issues

High-Quality Program

It's perfectly normal for three-year-olds to prefer playing alone or side-by-side with another child, and good teachers understand and support this behavior. They know that children this age aren't usually comfortable in big groups, and instead schedule small group activities with just a few.

Three-year-olds are just beginning to explore the wonders of friendship, and good teachers understand this may mean intense statements of "best friends" that evaporate after a few minutes. While good teachers encourage sharing, they also know that sometimes it's too much to expect a three-year-old to willingly give up a favorite toy.

Physical exercise is a very important part of preschool for three-year-olds, and good programs offer plenty of opportunity for running around outside to exercise the large muscle groups. Running and jumping are encouraged, and teachers supervise children riding tricycles or playing ball.

There is plenty of time to practice activities in a good preschool, and children are given the opportunity to repeat activities as much as they want until they have mastered the task.

Three-year-olds are encouraged to rest throughout the day, whenever they appear to be tired, because they can exhaust themselves—especially if they're trying to keep up with older students in a preschool.

In a good program, teachers give three-year-olds lots of opportunity to explore music and language. Children will be encouraged, in small groups, to recite nursery rhymes and poems, sing finger plays and other songs, and listen to music. They are given lots of simple rhythm instruments and allowed to make their own music. There will be opportunity for many movement and circle games, such as "London Bridge" or "ring-around-the-rosy."

Learning about their environment is important for three-year-olds, and good preschool programs provide materials that help these children exercise their natural curiosity. Expect to find blocks, dramatic play props, and any toy that opens, closes, or comes apart. The dramatic play corner is equipped with a variety of items, such as briefcases, adult clothes, telephones, cooking utensils, and dishes. Children love pretending to "go to work" and then "cook" dinner when they "come home."

One can always count on children's curiosity. Simple science activities such as flying kites or planting seeds are very popular at this age.

Three-year-olds are still developing their fine motor skills, but they'll have more control than two-year-olds. They may even name their drawings, but good teachers know that they won't necessarily be able to produce a picture that truly represents actual objects. Instead, art is seen as creative expression, and teachers won't mind if the picture doesn't "look like something."

Low-Quality Program

In a low-quality program, you'll see three-year-olds herded into large groups for most of the day, moving from one activity to the next with little opportunity for solitary exploration. Children are not allowed to leave large group activities.

Teachers tend to pair children up, autocratically deciding who might "work well" together and requiring that children maintain these relationships regardless of their own feelings.

You'll often hear "No running!" in a poorly run program, even outdoors when it's perfectly acceptable to run around. Poor programs offer little playground space or provide little in the way of interesting equipment that exercises young muscles.

Teachers emphasize repetition in a low-quality program, regardless of whether a child has any interest in the activity, or they refuse to allow a child to repeat an activity in which she's interested. This is unfortunate, because three-year-olds need plenty of opportunity to perfect skills and often enjoy repetitive practice.

Naptimes are either rigidly enforced or ignored and then children are scolded for being grouchy later in the day if they haven't been given an opportunity to rest.

In a low-quality program, children will be allowed to participate in music only in a large group, when they may be *required* to participate. Language and music opportunities are limited because teachers believe students will get too loud or silly.

You may find play props and blocks in a low-quality or poorly run program, but odds are the teachers will have definite ideas about how children should use these items and restrict play to that area of the room. You won't find sand or water play in these programs, because staff believe it's too messy. You also won't find many toys that can be taken apart, because staff won't want to have to spend so much time cleaning up.

It's inappropriate for a teacher to look at a drawing by a three-year-old and ask, "What is it?" They should not give the impression that only art that "looks like something" is acceptable. In a poorly run program, staff will teach art by requiring children to color inside the lines of coloring books or mimeographed sheets, or ask children to model identically a piece of art as exhibited by the teacher.

Environment

High-Quality Program

Much like in the toddler classroom, the environment should be child-friendly, with soft, warm colors, functionally divided areas, real life pictures at the children's eye level, and educational books on the shelves.

The walls are decorated with children's and other artwork. Posters and pictures show meaningful concepts such as easy-to-recognize situations, objects, or places—a fire truck, a beach, a birthday party.

Three-year-olds are ready for more challenging concepts. Literacy is one of them. Literacy begins with letter-recognition, and as many items as possible labeled and placed at the child's eye level.

The physical abilities of three-year-olds are greater than that of two-year-olds, and they may be bigger and require more space. This eager, active, and energetic bunch is ready to explore. The pictures on the walls, play props, and toys in general are more complex. So are their activities. For example, they will enjoy having plants in the room, and it will be an honor for each one of them to take part in watering it daily.

There is plenty of light in the classroom and there are no dark corners. The classroom is "homey" with many familiar objects such as clocks, wall calendars, and rocking chairs. Children follow simple rules about taking turns and sharing as they move freely and choose their activities.

Three-year-olds should have more choices in their classroom than two-year-olds. The number of play areas might increase, and this offers more opportunities for learning. Many schools introduce computers at this age. Music instruments and audio equipment are a must in this classroom.

Soft floor cushions, comfy chairs, and other rest areas are provided. There is a place for a quiet, private moment if needed.

Many children this age are fully toilet trained; smaller toilets and low sinks should be provided.

Low-Quality Program

The first thing you will notice in a low-quality program is bad lighting. Rooms are either darkened on purpose or lack daily or proper artificial lighting.

Your overall impression is that the space has not been adapted for children. Walls are covered with dark or unpleasantly bright colors. Most wall decorations are inappropriate and out of the sightline for children. Toys are either neatly put away out of children's reach or there is a lot of clutter, which reveals that there is either little or no activity in the classroom or that children are simply doing everything at the same time and do not have schedules and rules to follow.

The furniture is scattered without any particular order in mind, and rooms often look like runways or are too cramped. Because of all this, teachers can't properly control the groups of children or can't see them behind the furniture.

There is no space for art and music centers and no signs that language development (such as labeling) is encouraged. There aren't enough books and toys; consequently, children are bored and "pick" on each other.

Children are often forced to socialize all the time because there aren't cozy spaces where they can take a break. This is hard for them and there are lots of conflicts.

Toilets are inappropriately sized and not kept clean. The tables used for both eating and playing are not cleaned after each use.

Health and Safety

High-Quality Program

Teachers understand that good hygiene is a must. Children are taught proper hand-washing and brush their teeth after meals. They have their own sleeping mats or cots and never share sheets, pillows, or blankets.

There are plenty of paper tissues, and children are taught how to use them.

All trash cans have lids. Toys and bathrooms are disinfected daily. All hazardous materials are stored in a safe place, and all outlets are covered. Good teachers understand that three-year-olds may overestimate their own abilities and may often attempt physical activities beyond their stamina. This is particularly a problem if three-, four-, and five-year-olds share the classroom or a playground. Because the three-year-olds will try to model the behavior of their older friends, teachers will closely monitor all indoor and outdoor activities and will help ease inevitable frustrations if a three-year-old can't do something an older child can do. There will always be enough staff for supervising larger groups. The student-teacher ratio rules are strictly followed.

Low-Quality Program

Children are not taught good hygiene habits. Necessities like soap and paper towels are often missing, and children share personal items.

Teachers are not maintaining basic cleanliness in the classrooms. Broken and age-inappropriate toys are offered. Children get easily frustrated, bored, and even hurt if the toys are out of their age range or simply do not work properly.

You don't want to see staff being casual about supervision, especially in a multi-age preschool. Children are ignored when conflicts arise or told to fend for themselves. This often ends in accidents. Poorly prepared teachers will not find it necessary to immediately attend the children who were hurt, because some are considered to be "cry babies."

Parent-Teacher Interaction

High-Quality Program

Parents are informed about their children's progress on a daily basis. This is done in person, through notes or mandatory written daily reports, lesson plans, calendars, and/or newsletters. No matter what kind of message system the school creates, parents will know what is happening and will get a better sense of involvement. Personal messages and friendly daily chats between the teachers and parents are the best way to keep things on track. Good programs will follow this rule, and parents will be at ease if they know that they are supported in their concerns or wish to be actively involved in their children's upbringing.

Teachers are available for a phone call or an occasional quick meeting.

Low-Quality Program

Communication is poor, messages are lost, and parents do not know what is happening. There aren't any opportunities to exchange ideas or experiences.

Even though teachers might be willing to chat with parents, the issues might be overseen. Mistakes happen often, and the only person you might get the news from is the director. It is not pleasant for either children or their parents to show up on time for a field trip to the zoo a day earlier or later just because a typo in the announcement was not corrected.

The observations in this chapter are a quick rundown of what to look for and what to stay away from when looking for a quality preschool. Even so, they will give you a good idea of what is going on in preschool classrooms for children of this age and enable you to make the best choice you can make.

In the Next Chapter

In the next chapter, you'll learn what makes a quality preschool program for children aged four and five, and what specific strengths you can expect at this age.

Chapter 3

Spotting Quality:
Preschools for Ages
Four and Five

If you have a preschooler between ages four and five, you already know how important it is to prepare him for a good education. As school age approaches, you'll want your child to be independent, confident, friendly, and eager to learn and explore. All of these qualities can be nurtured in a top-quality preschool.

A good preschool for this age group should provide a good teacher, the opportunity for your child to freely choose activities, and enough time to finish a project.

By age 4, children can play board and card games and follow simple rules, may be able to recognize and name all primary colors, hop, walk down stairs with alternate feet, talk in 4- to 5-word sentences, sing songs, listen to stories, share things spontaneously, and count to 10. Speech should be fully understandable. They should understand some basic concepts such as numbers, size, weight, texture, distance, time, and position.

Youngsters this age are very talkative, enjoying serious discussions and asking lots of questions, including "How?" and "Why?" They are getting better at classifying objects and reasoning, but don't be alarmed if you notice their language includes silly words and profanity—this is typical for four-year-olds.

By age five, children can play cooperatively with other children, play board and card games and follow the rules, name all the primary colors, skip, sing songs, listen to stories, share things spontaneously, recognize letters of the alphabet, print letters, and know both their phone number and address. This is a time of growing independence, and children at this age want to be considered more responsible.

Teachers

Good preschool teachers know that different backgrounds and experiences mean that children don't learn the same things at the same pace, and that their understanding of the world they live in may not be identical. No two children this age should be expected to follow the same developmental timetable. Some youngsters may recognize lots of numbers but stumble over words; others can barely tie their shoes or button a coat. The curriculum should be flexible and adaptable for those children who are more advanced and those who may need additional help.

Teachers should also allow children to spend time alone in a quiet area. Preschools are highly social environments that can be very busy and sometimes quite noisy. Many children spend long hours in preschools, and from time to time every child feels overwhelmed and deserves a little rest or a change of pace. They should be allowed to cuddle with their favorite teddy bear or a blanket or just "read" books while resting on soft floor cushions.

Rely on your first impressions. Watch for the interaction between children and teachers, especially between a teacher and your child. Do the teachers talk to each child on the child's eye level? Are they cheerful and optimistic? Watch staff-to-staff interaction. Are they friendly with each other? Do they seem to communicate a lot, and how?

Pay attention to the teacher-child ratio. Obviously, the fewer th
ber of children per teacher, the more attention your child will get. Listen
and look around, but avoid fast conclusions. Remember, sometimes children do misbehave. They get bored, they fight, and they have tantrums.
You might not know the whole story when incidents occur, but the way
the staff solves these problems can provide worlds of information you
won't find in a brochure or a pamphlet. If you have a good feeling about
the place, it's never a bad idea to ask questions and come back to observe
some more.

Environment

Scan the rooms for basic cleanliness and safety. If the classroom is too
orderly, there might not be enough activities provided. Do children in the
classroom seem generally happy and busy with activities? Is the classroom
too noisy? A high noise level might indicate a lack of control.

A good classroom, no matter how small or large, should be divided
into "learning centers"—sections of the room where children should experience hands-on learning through play. There should be a center for
everyone. In most preschools, there are 8 to 10 centers, carefully arranged
so noisy spots are separated from quiet areas.

You will probably see an art corner, science area, library, music and
instrument centers, dramatic play area, a housekeeping area, building
blocks, table toys, and—yes—computers. Each of these centers plays a
tremendous role in a child's learning and has significant influence on the
daily routine of the classroom. If you're observing a classroom that doesn't
use centers, make sure that the materials described in this section are
available for the children to use every day.

Each learning center should be well organized. Materials should be
clean and in good condition, organized on shelves and labeled with pictures or descriptive word tags.

The number of materials available in each center will depend on the
age of the children in the class, but here's a good rule of thumb: For two-
year-olds, look for four materials per center; for five-year-olds, look for

at least six materials per center. A preschool should contain many of the following centers and materials:

- Math Center: Counting games, materials to count, graphs and charts, and number lines.

- Block Center: A full set of wooden blocks, cars and trucks, and small figures to add to block structures.

- Dramatic Play/"Pretend" Center: Dress-up clothes for boys and girls, a puppet theater, play food and dishes, toy stove or other appliances, dolls, and cribs.

- Prop boxes: Fire-fighting gear, restaurant play materials, and so on that enable children to experience different roles.

- Science Center: Plants, small animals, and natural objects to explore.

- Scoop and Pour: Cornmeal, rice, oatmeal, water, or other substances children can scoop and pour. Children use a variety of measuring cups and materials to scoop, which creates an educational experience.

- Fine Motor Center: Puzzles, Legos, games, stringing and lacing activities, and other materials.

- Art Center: Easels, paint, crayons, scissors, glue, paper, collage materials, markers, modeling clay, and other materials. Children should be able to help themselves (two-year-olds may need help).

- Music Center: Tapes or CDs and a player, musical instruments, books with words to the music, and scarves to dance to the music.

- Reading Center: A bookshelf full of age-appropriate books and a comfortable place to sit and read.

There should be plenty of room so that everyone can move around freely. The furniture should be low and carefully positioned to divide the room into sections, so the teacher should always be able to monitor the children during their individual activities. If, for instance, a group of children is sitting on the floor, the teacher should be able to see them over a low bookshelf.

Social/Emotional Development

One of the main goals of preschool is to teach children social skills such as getting along with peers and listening to adults other than their parents. Keep in mind that children develop at different rates. While every child is unique and will develop different personalities, there are some common behavioral traits among preschoolers this age.

Four- and five-year-olds are becoming more adept at interacting with the world around them. They tend to have lots of energy and may play aggressively. Their behavior can range from loud and adventurous to shy and dependent.

Most four-year-olds are very independent and want to do things alone. They still have difficulties sharing but understand the benefits of taking turns and can wait for longer periods of time. Simple board games and group play on the playground with clear and simple rules help them learn to cooperate.

Mood swings are common, and children may be aggressive and tend to brag a bit and be bossy. They can be very assertive but want friends and enjoy being with other children.

Children this age have very active imaginations and may have imaginary friends. They enjoy pretending to be important adults, such as mother or father, doctor or nurse, police officer or fire fighter.

By age five, children are becoming generally more cooperative and responsible than four-year-olds and are eager to please others and make them happy.

Children aged four and five enjoy more group activities because they have longer attention spans. They like making faces and being silly. Friendships may develop into cliques, and friends may come and go quickly. Preschool teachers for children this age are used to dealing with name-calling, swear words, and bathroom words.

Typical Activities

Children this age will spend most of their day playing and working with various materials, either alone or with other children. In a good preschool program, the children will not be bored. They should not be expected to sit still for long periods of time, and they should not all be doing the same things at the same time. Instead, they should have a choice of different activities throughout the day.

Teachers should be working with individual children, with small groups, or all children together at different times during the day. Teachers should be sensitive to each child's individual emotional, physical, and thinking differences, especially in mixed-age classrooms. For example, some younger children can follow older friends on the playground, but others get tired faster and really need their naps.

While they do well in group activities, many still need more individual attention and do better in smaller groups. With this in mind, good programs carefully plan daily schedules and classroom routines that allow for flexibility in accommodating all children in the classroom.

Teachers should carefully follow daily schedules, because children feel more comfortable with an established routine. They don't respond well to sudden dramatic changes and hectic schedules. They feel more confident about themselves in familiar situations and surroundings.

Of course, this doesn't mean that children shouldn't be exposed to new things and experiences. Rather, routine should accompany new experiences. A good preschool will allow freedom within an overall sense of structure.

Through carefully planned daily, weekly, or monthly lesson plans, children can practice skills they have previously gained while learning about something new. For example, if children are discussing their families with classmates, they should be able to exchange photos and familiarize themselves with many aspects of family life: size of a family, names of family members, cultural background, relationships, and so on.

Physical Activity

As children mature, gross motor skills, improved coordination and balance, and increased strength and endurance become the focus of physical development.

Children this age have better control in running, jumping, and hopping, but they tend to be clumsy. By age four, they should be able to gallop, skip, throw a ball overhand, and pump themselves on a swing.

Outdoor play is very important, so be sure the preschool you visit provides ample opportunity to get out and run around. Children should play outside every day, weather permitting, because their overall development greatly depends on their physical fitness.

By now, they have developed more small muscle control, so they can make representational pictures, such as drawings of animals, houses, and people. They can cut on a line with scissors, make designs, and write crude letters.

They like unzipping, unsnapping, and unbuttoning clothes, and they dress themselves. Although they like lacing their own shoes, most probably can't tie their shoes yet.

Toys

There are certain kinds of toys you should expect to find in a good preschool for four- and five-year-olds. Look for assortments of building blocks and other construction materials and lots of boxes filled with play props and dress-up clothes. Dramatic play is the biggest part of every child's learning. They love role-playing, dress-up, and manipulating housekeeping objects. This helps strengthen basic communication skills as they enjoy playing "families" and "school." Youngsters this age also love putting together a play or a puppet show for friends or parents. Puzzles, matching games, pegboards, and other constructive table toys are essential. A good selection of favorite board games is an excellent way of introducing fair competition to children and working with them in small groups.

Look at the toys carefully: Are there enough toys for everyone to avoid conflicts? Are the toys age-appropriate, interactive, up-to-date, and educational? Are they within children's reach?

Books

You should see lots of picture books with topics children this age can relate to. Children this age are capable of understanding many complex issues. They are also developing a sense of humor and empathy. Families, friendships, and getting along, for instance, are very popular topics. Teachers should be reading to children individually and in group settings throughout the day.

Art

Art should be an important part of the classroom for children this age. Art materials should include paint, glue, glitter, scissors, modeling clay, markers, and so on.

Look around during your visit. Are the walls covered with lots of colorful artwork? Children's art should be an important part of the overall room décor, and it should be displayed at the child's eye level.

But art is more than just their own scribbles and doodles—teachers also should begin to introduce classical and modern art and let the children discuss freely what they see.

Music

Most children this age love music—both listening to good music and performing on their own. Good preschools shouldn't limit their musical offerings to a couple of battered Raffi tapes—they should provide a wide variety of music choices, ranging from classical to international to contemporary.

It's a fact that children this age enjoy movement and singing. They love to express themselves freely, and good classrooms will have enough space for dancing and plenty of musical instruments, such as small drums, tambourines, cymbals, sleigh bells, and kazoos.

Communication

Children this age are great talkers and questioners and love to use words in rhymes, nonsense, and jokes. You should notice that lots of objects around the classroom are labeled, along with examples of the children's efforts at printing letters and dictated stories. This is the way children best familiarize themselves with language and spelling.

Most 4-year-olds can say approximately 1,500 different words, and may put together 4 to 5 words in a sentence. They will ask questions constantly and may know most primary colors. By the age of 5, most children can say approximately 2,000 words and may put together 6 to 8 words into a sentence. They may recognize shapes and name the days of the week.

Mathematics

Numbers should also be part of the curriculum and should be taught in the context of everyday experiences. For example, a good way to learn basic numbers is to count beads while working on an art project or adding up the number of glasses while helping to set tables for snacks or lunch.

By age five, most children should be able to name coins and money and understand commands with multiple instructions.

Science

Good preschools should have a science area decorated with live plants— and if possible, a live pet such as fish, a rabbit, or a guinea pig. Taking care of the school pet helps children learn responsibility and nurtures a love of nature. Having an animal around the room can also relax children during the day. Watering plants or feeding a pet are usually favorite activities in a preschool classroom for children this age.

Cooking

Children this age appreciate any opportunity to don an apron and cook up a snack, and good preschools provide lots of these experiences. Children enjoy mixing, measuring, and, of course, tasting their products—and it's also a great way to work on numbers and other math concepts.

Guidelines for Ages Four and Five: High-Quality and Low-Quality Programs

As you prepare to visit preschools for your four- or five-year-old child, there are certain things you're going to want to watch for that illustrate a good program—and some things you don't want to see. Following are some guidelines that will help you know what to look out for, with details about both good and poor preschool programs for four- and five-year-olds.

Your experiences will most likely coincide with the following descriptions, and you will feel prepared for a quick "inspection."

Teacher Qualifications

High-Quality Program

In a good preschool, teachers have studied early childhood education and are qualified to work with four- and five-year-olds. They have experience with this age group. There are no more than 10 children per adult, and class size is not larger than 20 in a good program. This combination allows for individualized, age-appropriate programs.

Low-Quality Program

In a low-quality program, four- and five-year-olds are taught by teachers without any specialized training. Because older children can function in larger groups, poorly run preschools may allow classes for 4- and 5-year-olds to be as large as classes in elementary school—25 to 30 pupils per teacher.

Teacher-Child Interaction

High-Quality Program

Interaction between the child and the teacher is positive. The teacher speaks respectfully to children in a soft voice and at their eye level most of the time. Children follow directions without feeling frustrated or uneasy. They are encouraged to make choices, resolve conflicts, and come up with solutions on their own.

Teachers are cheerful and optimistic and always ready for a smile. They do not raise their voices unless there is an emergency.

Low-Quality Program

Teachers are impatient and ignore or scold children. They raise their voices often. They seem frustrated and never smile. Children do not feel at ease when asking questions and seem to fear the teachers.

Curriculum Issues

Exactly what is being taught in a program for four- and five-year-olds has become controversial in light of the demand for formal education of very young children. Too many people are calling for narrowly defined academic skills and increased reliance on standardized tests to determine who will be enrolled in preschool programs.

In response to pressure to show that children are "really learning" in preschool, many programs have begun to emphasize paper-and-pencil activities that are simply inappropriate for four- and five-year-olds.

Instead, the best way to tell whether a preschool for children this age is a good one is to decide whether the program is developmentally appropriate, according to the National Association for the Education of Young Children. (For details, see beginning of this chapter.)

High-Quality Program

In a good preschool, teachers recognize that each child is an individual and develops according to his or her own timetable. Different learning styles are accepted, and the program is altered to accommodate everyone's learning style. Good teachers understand that all developmental areas are important—intellectual, social, emotional, and physical.

Good teachers allow children to select their own activities in a variety of learning areas, including art, music, drama, science, and math.

Good programs know that standardized testing is inappropriate for children this age and make decisions about enrollment or remediation based on observations, not test scores. Developmental assessments are used to plan school programs and identify children with special needs.

Low-Quality Program

In a poorly prepared program, children are evaluated using only standardized tests, and everyone is expected to be able to do the same tasks and achieve the same skill level. The teacher inappropriately focuses on a child's intellectual development and ignores all other areas of development.

Inappropriate programs require teachers to direct all of the children's learning activities, deciding what everyone will do and when. The teacher tends to perform all the activities or experiments, so children don't get a chance to participate.

Inappropriate programs rely on standardized testing for enrollment and remedial decisions. Little effort is made to assess a child's developmental readiness from observation.

Environment

High-Quality Program

Busy classrooms are good classrooms; if you don't see children wandering aimlessly, you must be in a good preschool. Children are engaged in all kinds of activities and are freely moving around choosing materials and props. There seem to be plenty of toys and other learning materials for everyone. The room is orderly, and the toys are neatly put away after use. Children talk to each other and to teachers and seem happy.

Low-Quality Program

One of the first signs of a low-quality program is the noise level. A high noise level reveals lack of control and could overly stimulate the children.

Number of toys is limited, and when there is an activity offered, all children must participate. There is no place for children to rest during the day. Books are missing pages, and toys are missing parts.

If the children are scattered about, without anything else to do but run around, you don't want to observe further.

Health and Safety

High-Quality Program

The classroom is big enough to serve a large number of children, and there is enough supervision. The room is clean and well lighted. There is no clutter, and fire exits are visible. Bathrooms are kept clean and are easily accessible to children. Everything has its place; if not in use, all toys and materials are neatly stored where children can easily reach them.

Low-Quality Program

Children can be seen even outside the classroom, but it might not be easy to find a teacher. If the classrooms and the bathrooms appear unclean, they probably are. Seeing bottles with disinfecting solutions within children's reach is not a good sign either.

The exits are not clearly marked, and the toys are everywhere. Children are not taught basics, like personal hygiene and cleaning up after themselves. The room is full of dark corners, and the air is stifling.

Parent-Teacher Interactions

High-Quality Program

Good teachers enjoy working in a partnership with parents, eagerly sharing all information and communicating on a daily basis.

Low-Quality Program

In an inappropriate program, teachers talk to parents only when there is a problem and tend to dismiss parents with the idea that teachers are the experts and, therefore, know the child best.

It may take some time, but by carefully studying the descriptions of high- and low-quality programs offered in this chapter, you will become adept at telling the difference between the two.

In the Next Chapter

Now that you've gotten a good idea of what a typical program might look like for different age groups, in the next chapter we'll discuss the beginning of the preschool quest. You'll learn how to find out what's out there, check references, evaluate the curriculum, and learn more about the basics of each program you investigate.

Chapter 4

Starting Your
Preschool Quest

You should start your quest for a preschool early—but just how early depends on where you live and how competitive the preschools are in your town. Some parents can start looking a year or so before their child is ready for preschool, whereas for others, applying at birth isn't too early for the best schools in the biggest cities. If you have reason to believe your top choice is at all competitive, then you'll need to apply to more than one in case you don't get your first choice.

In general, however, most preschools conduct registration for the fall during the preceding winter. In order to meet possible deadlines, be prepared to decide on a preschool six to eight months before your child begins.

In Chapter 1 we discussed the basic philosophies of a variety of preschools. Now you're going to have to do some research to find two or three preschools you think might work for your family.

What's Important to You?

First you need to figure out what is important to you. Here are some aspects to consider.

Convenience

Do you need a preschool located within a few minutes of your job, or would a facility closer to your home be more convenient? Does the school offer full-time or part-time-only attendance?

Curriculum

What kinds of curriculum are you interested in—heavy on the math and science, or a program that includes more artistic activities such as dancing and puppets? Are you looking for a specific approach to learning such as a Waldorf or Montessori program? Do you want a school that emphasizes religious instruction?

Philosophy

Do you want a child-centered school where activities are determined by the children and their interests, or a teacher-directed program that focuses on academics?

Your Child's Personality

Also keep in mind the personal characteristics of your child. Some children are more comfortable in large groups than others and will do well in large programs. On the other hand, if your child takes a long time to warm up in a crowd, you may want to look for a small-scale preschool program.

Some children can start in preschool and hit the ground running. Other, more quiet or sensitive children may typically be more reserved, holding back and sizing up a situation before plunging ahead. If this sounds like your child, it's vital that you find a program where the teachers make an effort to involve children while not pushing them intensely to adjust on the first day. Some kids simply take longer to make the transition.

Because children's temperaments vary, you need to keep your child's level of comfort in mind. Whereas most active, outgoing children may react positively to situations where lots of activities are going on within one area, other, quieter children may feel more comfortable and safe in a quieter, more structured preschool. If your child is quiet and shy, she might to do better with a smaller group.

Consistency

Some children are born free spirits who don't seem to mind when they eat, play, or sleep. Others crave schedules and function best only within a comforting structure. These children eat, sleep, and play in very organized ways. Because consistency is important in the preschool years, most programs follow a daily schedule that children craving regularity will find comforting.

However, free spirits might have trouble adjusting to a schedule. If you suspect that your child might have problems adjusting to the new schedule at school, it's a good idea to find a teacher who's flexible enough to let your child slowly acclimate to a new schedule.

Energy Level

Some children seem to have a never-ending supply of energy, constantly flitting from one activity to another. If your child seems especially fond of vigorous physical activities and outdoor play, you may want to ensure that the preschool provides good outdoor space and equipment.

If you notice that a particular preschool doesn't provide many opportunities for running around and exercising, it's probably not the school for you.

Sensory Level

It's also important to determine your child's sensory level. Many young children seem to crave commotion and, therefore, thrive in a busy preschool. Others have a lower tolerance for noise, lights, and activity, and become easily overwhelmed by chaos. If your child seems sensitive to her surroundings, you might want to look for a facility with quiet areas where your child can retreat for some private time. It's also important that teachers understand the different needs for activity and quiet.

After giving these questions some thought, you'll be able to zero in on the kind of preschool that best fits your needs. Make a list of your priorities so you can keep your preferences straight as you evaluate programs.

Do Your Research

You can find out a lot more about good preschools by asking friends and neighbors than by checking the Yellow Pages. But don't stop there—ask the experts, too.

If you don't happen to have an early childhood educator in the family, check out the Childcare Aware hot line at 1-800-424-2246. This number can link you up with your local child-care referral agency, which can refer you to licensed and accredited preschools nearby.

Once you have the names of several preschools, call the National Association for the Education of Young Children (NAEYC) at 1-800-424-2460 to find out if they've given accreditation to any of the preschools you've selected.

The NAEYC is the country's most trusted preschool accreditation organization; their accreditation ensures that a program has surpassed the state's minimum licensing requirements. If they've accredited the program, you should have some confidence in the quality of the preschool.

If they haven't accredited any of the programs, don't panic. Many perfectly good preschools (especially smaller ones) don't apply for accreditation. NAEYC accredits only a fraction of the schools in the country.

Check out the Internet (addresses for all these websites are listed in Appendix A):

- CareGuide features extensive state-by-state directories of U.S. preschools.

- KidCare also offers state-by-state directories of U.S. preschools.
- NAEYC also offers a searchable database of accredited preschools.
- National Association of Family Child Care offers a website with guidelines and contact information.

Call the Preschools

Next, call the preschools you've chosen and ask them to send you any brochures or other information. Ask for printed details about the school's philosophy and curriculum, and request a copy of the daily schedule.

Make certain you are comfortable with what is stated. By studying these materials closely, you should be able to determine the school's educational philosophy and decide if it matches your own.

You may find yourself drawn to the preschool that chooses to highlight children swinging from bars on the playground in its brochure instead of one focusing on rows of children staring fixedly at a bank of computers.

Take the brochure with you on your first visit (see Chapter 5), and be on the lookout for any discrepancies between what you've been told and what you observe.

Check References

Any school should be happy to give you a list of past and present references. Before you visit, get a list of references—and call some of the parents on the list. Don't just ask whether they like the preschool—be specific and ask what exactly they like about the program and what they don't. If their child no longer attends that preschool, find out why.

If you're wary of the names the school gives you (they probably won't give you names of unhappy parents), stop by during afternoon pick-up and approach other parents then. Ask them about their experiences with the school. Consider asking some of the following questions:

- What is your overall impression of the school?
- How does the teacher discipline your child?
- Does your child enjoy the preschool experience?
- How does the teacher respond to you as a parent?
- Is the teacher respectful of your values and culture?
- Would you recommend the preschool without reservation?

But remember—you and your child should be the final judge of the school. Unhappy parents may simply have had a personality conflict with the preschool director or with a teacher, or perhaps that program just wasn't suited to that child. Just because one family didn't like the preschool doesn't mean it's a bad choice.

Next, call your local child-care resource and referral program or licensing office and ask what regulations preschools in your area should meet and whether there is a record of complaints about the preschool you are considering. You also might want to contact your local office of the Better Business Bureau to see whether any complaints have been filed against the school or its teachers.

Evaluate the Curriculum

Some preschools (such as Montessori or the Waldorf school) have clearly delineated educational philosophies that will probably not vary much from one program to the next, but other programs will have more diversity. What's most important in any program is that the teachers encourage independence and inspire your child's individuality and creativity.

Schedules

Good schools plan and implement a learning program based on careful and thorough observations of each child's individual needs, developmental stages, and progress. The best preschools have daily schedules that include plenty of time for physical activity, quiet time (including regular reading sessions), group programs, socializing, crafts, individual activities, meals, snacks, and free time. TV and videos should not play a big part in your child's day. A well-thought-out curriculum stimulates your child's development and makes daily life more fun.

Activities

An effective preschool program includes a variety of activities, including free-choice activities and small group times; quiet periods and active times; many short activities and a few longer ones to increase the child's attention span; and careful planning to develop the child socially, emotionally, physically, and intellectually.

Letters/Numbers

In preschool, teachers can start helping children learn concepts like letters and numbers in an everyday context by counting toys, cutting out pictures of things that start with the different letters of the alphabet, and so on. But don't rate a school based on how many numbers and letters they teach—remember that preschoolers aren't ready for a rigorous academic program.

Balance

A developmentally appropriate curriculum focuses on all areas of the developing child, including social, emotional, thinking, and movement skills. It should be based on play and offer a balance of child-directed creative play with more structured activities. The environment should feel warm and friendly, with appropriate materials to support growth and learning in all areas.

The curriculum should change over time so that your child can have the chance to try something new, and it should be adjusted to match each child's ability and skill levels.

If you have more than one child, you know very well that no two are exactly alike. Good schools recognize this and avoid using a cookie-cutter approach to their curriculum. Of course, attention to individual student needs depends greatly on the ratio of students to teachers—which is why the child-to-teacher ratio is so important.

The lower the ratio, the better the environment for learning. The ideal range is six to eight preschoolers to one teacher. However, this is probably the lowest ratio you will encounter in schools with a capacity of 60 to 80 children. Smaller schools will likely have lower ratios.

In a quality classroom, you'll see that the teacher provides acceptable ways for the active child to keep moving and learning. There will be preparation time for transitions and chances to jump into activities or watch comfortably from the sidelines. The activities and techniques fit all types of children.

Communicate

If you have any questions that might pertain to individualizing the curriculum to meet your own child's needs, your first visit will be a good time to ask.

Remember, the more open you are in communicating your needs, the more likely the school will be able to satisfy your requests. Administrators aren't mind readers—and good schools often appreciate the input.

Admission

Each preschool has its own admissions and eligibility policies. It's important to find out about these requirements early. Many centers give preference to siblings of children already enrolled. This is something worth keeping in mind if you already have more than one child or are planning a bigger family.

Some schools might provide attendance schedules they believe are developmentally and age appropriate. For example, some programs for 2½-year-olds limit attendance to 2 hours a day.

In a few instances, schools require that a parent accompany the child, because they believe that separation anxiety inhibits quality learning. Other preschool programs won't allow parents to stay with their children even for a few minutes. Some will only accept 2½-year-olds who are toilet trained; others are more flexible.

In some instances, three- and four-year-olds are expected to be socially experienced, and you might find that these schools have a low tolerance for individual adjustment issues.

To avoid confusion, be sure to ask for the school's admission and enrollment requirements in writing. Sometimes this information is included in a handbook, or it may be a separate document. Either way, it's best to have your own copy so you can review specific requirements leisurely at home.

Preenrollment

You may find that you are required to preenroll your child in a preschool program. If this is the case, you'll likely be required to complete a battery of forms, including the child's developmental history, a health certificate, acknowledgment of school policies, notarized emergency medical forms, proof of childhood immunizations, and an authorization for your child to be taken on field trips. A nonrefundable fee is usually associated with the preenrollment.

Once the child has been accepted, the school will usually require a security deposit, which can often equal up to two weeks' or a month's worth of tuition.

The Ground Rules

Before you schedule your first visit, try to find out some of the basic rules of the preschool. A good preschool shouldn't feel like a prison camp. For example, staff should be flexible enough to let you pick up and drop off your child at different times. Still, the school should also have clearly established written regulations about basics like operating hours, holidays, and emergencies. That way, you know the staff takes its responsibility seriously.

There is a whole range of policies the preschool has probably already established. Most of these items should be included in a detailed handbook provided to parents. If they're not, ask.

It's important to know what's expected of you before the first day of class. Go through these rules carefully, and don't be afraid to ask questions, even if you don't bring them up in your meeting and have to call later.

Most preschools have policies about the following:

- Hours of operation
- Closings
- Drop-off and pick-up procedures
- Sick-child policy
- Parking issues
- School-family communication
- Holidays
- Meal guidelines
- Drop-in policies
- Absences, withdrawal, and dismissal policies
- Medication administration

Hours of Operation

Hours of operation means the earliest time the school is open through the latest time you can pick up your child. If a school states that the hours of operation are from 7 A.M. through 6 P.M., you may bring in or pick up your up child at any time during these hours.

However, in some preschools hours of operation differ. For example, their official hours might be from 9 A.M. to 3 P.M. but they will be open for a couple extra hours in the morning and afternoon. These extra hours are for an extra charge. Even though a couple dollars per hour can seem affordable, think twice. It's hard to believe, but a few dollars twice a day add up quickly.

Closings

Every preschool has an in-house calendar, which is created to inform all parents about upcoming events, important dates, and, of course, about closings. Holiday closings may vary depending on the type of preschool you choose. Naturally, if your preschool is an extension of a religious organization, expect to have all related holidays off. On the other hand, many schools remain open for all major winter holidays, but the services they offer might be different than usual: There may be an extra charge, shorter hours, and so on.

It might suit you that school is open on some national holidays, but they might close for a week or two for a spring break. Ask for the calendar; it is useful to know about this ahead of time. This means that sometimes you may have to plan your vacations to coincide with the school's closings.

Schools also close for other reasons—such as for staff development purposes. Teachers clean the classrooms, sort the equipment and toys, plan activities, attend lectures and courses, and so on. Such a closing could happen any time of the year and last for a couple days. First aid and CPR are just some of the required courses and teachers must renew their certificates periodically. Preschools are very busy and this is their time to improve the ways they serve the children.

Drop-Off and Pick-Up Procedures

Pay particularly careful attention to drop-off and pick-up procedures. Schools usually have rigid rules about timely pick-up of children, and many schools penalize late parents by charging a fine for each minute you're late after closing time. This can often add up to a hefty figure! Good schools will stick to this policy, so don't be late.

Unless someone else has been authorized, only parents can pick up children. This policy is for your child's protection, and you can expect the preschool to be quite firm on it. You should also know that preschools will not release a child to parents or guardians whom they believe to be in any way intoxicated or under the influence of illegal drugs.

Drop-off time is mostly personal preference and can depend on your needs, but be sensitive to your child's need for consistency and the teacher's efforts to maintain it. Be familiar with daily schedules. For instance, walking in at the middle of book reading or a group discussion can be very unpleasant for your child and is also disrupting to the class. Also, if the science class starts at 9 A.M., make sure your child is there. You want your child to participate from the beginning and not feel left out.

Sick-Child Policy

Look for a school with a strict sick-child policy. Find out which symptoms and illnesses mean your child has to stay home and for how long. It may seem inconvenient if you have to miss an important meeting because your child has pinkeye, but it's only fair to the other children. A good preschool helps cut down on illness by requiring everyone to have current immunizations and regular check-ups.

Unfortunately, this is often not enough. Children are known to spread germs fast and easily infect each other. Even in the well-disinfected classroom, one unnoticed sneeze on an often-used puzzle or a doll can cause lots of absences. The only way preschools can protect children from large illness outbreaks is to strictly adhere to a couple ground rules.

Many very contagious illnesses begin with some commonly known symptoms. Preschools may tolerate an occasional runny nose or a mild cough but expect a call from the school if …

- Your child's fever is or exceeds 100°F.
- Your child vomits, has diarrhea, or has green nose discharge.
- Your child has persistent and severe cough.
- Your child develops an unusual rash.

In case of a serious injury or other health and safety emergencies, the school is obligated to notify you immediately. Make sure all your contact numbers in the school's records are correct and up to date.

You may be asked to pick your child up as fast as possible, but the usual time frame is about an hour. Remember that a sick child needs a lot of attention, and teachers might have a difficult time caring for other children in the class.

Parking Issues

Parking can be a big issue. Schools in crowded urban areas struggle with lack of adequate parking. This can result in a long walk to the car with a child who can be cranky and tired, and it can be an unexpected expense if you get lots of parking tickets.

Ask if there is a convenient place to park while you pick up your child. Know the parking situation ahead of time.

School-Family Communication

Good preschools should offer checklists and other daily observation forms that help teachers keep careful records on each child's progress each day. Better schools will create forms that allow teachers to keep careful and confidential records of individual students; these can be easily shared with parents and administrators as needed.

Ask to see some samples of these forms when you visit, so you can assess the kind of individualized attention the school provides.

Holidays

Holidays at preschools are great opportunities to celebrate cultural diversity. The better schools will be sensitive about celebrating religious and nonreligious holidays in an unbiased, nonjudgmental way that creates a learning experience for all.

Most schools will usually honor parents' requests for their children not to participate in activities they deem unsuitable and will provide alternative activities during that time. If you feel that a particular holiday might present a problem for you, be sure to ask ahead of time and find out what other options the school offers.

Meal Guidelines

Find out if the school has any guidelines about food that you send in with your child. Some may require you to pack only nutritious foods, which is a good sign—preschools that don't care whether parents restrict candy or other sweets may not have your child's best interests at heart.

If the school does have a food plan, find out what it serves at meal and snack times. Does it encourage healthy eating habits and include all the food groups?

Drop-In Policies

If a preschool doesn't encourage you to stop by unannounced at any time, chances are there may be something to hide. A great preschool will not just allow you to visit—they will welcome you to become part of their community by helping with activities, accompanying the children on field trips, and so on.

Absences, Withdrawals, and Dismissal Policies

Be certain to check the school's rules and regulations about absences. Oftentimes, a phone call can save you from complications. In the event of a longer illness, if you're going on vacation, or you just want to stay at home with your child, always notify the school. Some preschools require prior notice if a child won't be attending the following day so they can plan appropriately.

Most preschools have firm withdrawal and dismissal policies and require adequate advance notice if you wish to leave the program within a reasonable amount of time. Generally, all schools require a two- to four-week notice. It takes time to smoothly transition another child from the program into your child's spot or get a new student. Chances are that better programs have long waiting lists and will quickly fill the spot.

Grounds for dismissal from a preschool vary, but they are often based on factors including the following:

- Behavior in a child that is threatening to others
- Repeatedly bringing in a sick child
- Failure to pay tuition promptly
- Repeated late pick-ups
- A child's special developmental needs
- Failure to notify school about longer absences

Medication Administration

Once you have decided to enroll your child into a preschool, you will have to provide some health information. Along with a health certificate from your child's pediatrician, you will be asked to fill out a developmental history form. This form is confidential and contains pertinent questions about your child's health and overall development. It is important for the staff to know about your child's allergies or chronic illness.

If your child has an ongoing health condition and needs his or her medication during the day, you will have to sign one or two consent forms, which will enable the staff to administer the medication. This is a standard procedure.

In case of an occasional need for antibiotics, you will also be asked to sign a form. Good programs will refuse to administer any over-the-counter medications such as cough syrup, topical ointments, or a fever medicine without your signature.

Most important, the school should provide a safe, locked-up place for the medicine your child is taking.

Signing an emergency medical treatment consent form is probably one of the first forms you will sign upon enrollment. Accidents can happen anytime and anywhere. Schools must be authorized by parents to administer emergency treatment and/or take children to the nearest hospital in case parents cannot be reached right away.

Licenses and Accreditation

All preschools need to be licensed, but not all preschools are accredited.

Requirements for a State License

Because the government classifies preschools as daycare centers rather than educational institutions, they have to meet the same licensing requirements as daycare centers.

However, keep in mind that a license isn't necessarily a guarantee of quality—it just shows that the facility has met the minimum health, safety, and teacher training standards set by the state.

In some states, having a license means only that a preschool has registered as a business; in others, it means a preschool has passed stringent requirements. In any case, you should ask to see the preschool's license when you visit to make sure it's at least up to date and check to see what it takes to get one in your state.

You can check the NAEYC website to see a state-by-state roundup of preschool license requirements. You can also check a preschool's license by calling your state or county social services department. Remember, preschools are classified as daycare centers and have to meet the same licensing requirements daycares do. In other words, don't go to the Department of Education for information on preschools.

NAEYC Accreditation

The National Association for the Education of Young Children (NAEYC) is the only national organization with the authority to grant accreditation for early childhood programs. This accreditation is one of the most concrete pieces of evidence that you have identified a recognized quality program. Like the proverbial Good Housekeeping Seal of Approval, accreditation from the NAEYC means that the selected school is committed to excellence and has passed a battery of tests and stringent evaluations including a thorough self-evaluation.

As of this writing, 7,600 programs serving more than 685,000 children have achieved NAEYC accreditation, and another 8,300 programs are in the process.

Child-care programs must be in operation for at least one year before being able to apply to the National Academy of Early Childhood Programs, a NAEYC division. Although accreditation isn't a guarantee that a preschool is right for your child, in general, if you find one with the NAEYC stamp of approval, it's a reliable sign of quality.

So far, the NAEYC has accredited only a fraction of the more than 96,000 U.S. licensed preschools. (Remember, however, that the accreditation process can take up to a year and cost hundreds of dollars, which is often the reason so few preschools have become accredited.)

Many more preschools have applied or are seriously considering going through the process of accreditation. This is a clear and very positive sign that many early childhood educators have recognized the need for quality standards in child care.

Accreditation Criteria

Candidate programs must undergo an extensive self-study based on criteria outlined by the academy, plus a series of inspections, validations, interviews, and reviews by professionally recognized educators. Even though every aspect of the school's operation is under scrutiny, the greatest emphasis is placed on staff-child interaction and the developmental value of the curriculum. In other words, the preschool is being judged mostly on what is really going on in the classroom and how this activity affects the children.

The entire accreditation process might take anywhere from nine months to one year. If the school passes these rigorous tests, its accreditation is valid for three years only. After that, it must undergo the process again.

Successfully accredited programs are very proud of their achievement. Often, one of the first things you'll notice on their brochures, stationery, or marketing materials is the Academy's insignia (a torch). You may also see the certificate of accreditation prominently featured on the entrance wall.

What If a Preschool Isn't Accredited?

Lack of accreditation does *not* mean you should avoid a program. Although accredited programs have clearly achieved a level of recognized excellence, not every accredited school may be right for you and your child's individual needs.

Many schools continue to maintain excellent standards without the NAEYC seal of approval. More likely, they are slowly realizing that this recognition is very important in reassuring parents and communities that their children are in good hands. It is up to you to do much of the homework yourself.

If the school you are visiting is not accredited, ask administrators if they are planning to do so. Many schools will significantly revamp their programs to meet these high standards.

For more information on NAEYC and/or accreditation, visit their website at www.naeyc.org.

Cost

You've finally reached the bottom line. The reality today is that preschool education is not cheap—especially good preschool education. It's still true that you get what you pay for, and you should assume that the cost of preschool is definitely linked to the quality of the program.

And remember that the younger your child, the higher the tuition. This is because younger children require more personalized attention, and quality schools always maintain appropriate teacher-student ratios for this purpose. The good news: As your child gets older, the costs gradually go down.

With the exception of Head Start, most preschool fees are about the same as the prices charged by daycare centers, though few preschools will cost as much as full-day care for an infant. Depending on where you live and the quality of the preschool, costs range from $4,000 to $10,000 per year (that's $333 to $833 monthly), according to the Child Care Information Exchange.

The cost will depend on how much time your child spends at preschool; obviously, a full-day, five-day-a-week program will be much more expensive than a class that meets just once or twice a week for a few hours.

Most preschools offer an installment plan, but keep in mind that, usually, the more quickly you pay the tuition in full (such as in two installments rather than monthly), the cheaper it will be for you. Many schools charge interest if the tuition payments are spread out over a period of months. Other schools offer weekly and monthly payments. Whatever the arrangement, be sure to ask about your options.

Some schools will provide information about tuition assistance to qualified parents. All tuition information should also be provided in writing. Be sure to ask about it if it isn't included in the parent handbook.

Parent-run cooperative preschools generally cost less—but they require more of your time.

Join the Queue ...

Once you are close to making a decision, contact the school of your choice and find out what you need to do to enroll your child. Most schools register students in the early spring for the upcoming fall. There may be additional screenings before your child will be accepted. You may need to put your child on a waiting list.

Some of the best preschools in big cities have waiting lists, while perfectly good schools in more suburban or rural areas are a snap to get into.

If the preschool of your dreams isn't available, don't give up. Add your child's name to the waiting list. But don't put all your eggs in one basket—apply to more than one school so you'll have other options. Don't hesitate to be on lists for two or more of your top choices.

Be aware, however, that once a school has notified you of an opening, you usually have a limited time to accept. It is common to pay a deposit months in advance to hold your child's place.

In the Next Chapter

Now that you've learned how to do the basic research, in the next chapter we'll discuss what to look for during the actual tour of a preschool and how to identify a superior program.

Chapter 5

Your First Visit

"When I walked into my daughter's preschool and saw the fabulous setup, I wanted to go there myself," remembers Susan, a Pennsylvania mom. "The place had a miniature grocery store with check-out counters, a construction loft, an indoor playhouse, a pretend hospital corner, even a big wooden fire engine with hats and coats. And the teachers were so warm and friendly. I knew right away this was the place."

You can weed out some undesirable or overly expensive programs just by talking to other parents on the phone, but only a visit to the preschool will provide the kind of details you'll need to determine if it's right for your child.

Keep in mind that what your best friend loves about her preschool might not work for your child. Choosing a preschool is a very personal decision. Trust your gut reaction: If you love the idea of leaving your child at a particular school, it's probably the right place for you.

Make the Appointment

You'll want to meet the teacher and director, watch their interaction with children, and check out the physical space. Here's a checklist to help you remember what to ask when you call to make an appointment to visit:

- Is there an opening for my child?
- What hours and days are you open, and where are you located?
- How much does care cost? Is financial assistance available?
- How many children are in your care?
- What age groups do you serve?
- Do you provide transportation?
- Do you provide meals (breakfast, lunch, dinner, snacks)?
- Are you accredited?
- When can I come to visit?

Once you've made appointments to see a number of preschools, have set the dates, and gotten time off work, you'll want to make the most of the tours you're about to undertake.

You'll want to make this first visit without your child so you are not interrupted or distracted as you observe classes and ask questions. Of course, your child's opinion matters, but you and your spouse should be the ones to select the school.

Do the preliminary search and visits on your own, and bring your child with you only when you're certain of your choice.

The Tour Begins

When you arrive at the school to begin the visit, give yourself time to get a feeling for the classroom's general atmosphere and the extent to which children appear comfortable and involved. A good educational climate is usually indicated by friendliness among the staff and children. When you walk in the door, you should be greeted by the teacher or administrator. Are they warm and welcoming? Do they seem pleased to see you?

Now, here's what to expect once you've arrived. You'd be surprised how many preschools follow a similar schedule. Here's a typical schedule for what you could expect in a half-day program:

8 to 8:15 A.M.:	Arrival and greetings.
8:15 to 8:30 A.M.:	Circle time. Weather and calendar, discuss plans for the day and new activities and theme concepts.
8:30 to 9:15 A.M.:	Exploration time. Children may choose from all the learning centers and special activities available. In some programs, they may also have the choice of outdoor activities.
9:15 to 9:25 A.M.:	Clean up and wash hands.
9:25 to 9:35 A.M.:	Snack.
9:35 to 10:10 A.M.:	Music, movement, and dramatic play.
10:10 to 10:45 A.M.:	Playground activities.
10:45 to 11 A.M.:	Story, review of day's activities.
11 to 11:30 A.M.:	Lunch.
11:30 A.M.:	Dismissal.

The Basics

Children in a good preschool are usually not easily distracted by visitors and should continue to be absorbed in their work or play. When children rush toward visitors and clamor for attention, abandoning their activities, it indicates that their activities aren't stimulating or interesting the children enough.

Are you comfortable? Do you hear the sounds of excited, happy children, or is the atmosphere oppressive and too quiet? Are children in their rooms and occupied, or are they aimlessly wandering around the rooms?

The National Association for the Education of Young Children (NAEYC) suggests that you look for these 10 signs of a good preschool classroom:

1. Children spend most of their time playing and working with materials or other children, not wandering aimlessly or sitting quietly for long periods of time.

2. Children have access to various activities throughout the day. Look for assorted building blocks and other construction materials, props for pretend play, picture books, paints and other art materials, and table toys such as matching games, pegboards, and puzzles.

3. Children should not all be doing the same thing at the same time. Teachers work with individual children, small groups, and the whole group at different times during the day—they don't spend all their time with the whole group.

4. The classroom is decorated with children's original artwork, their own writing with invented spelling, and stories dictated by children to teachers.

5. Children learn numbers and the alphabet in the context of their everyday experiences. The natural world of plants and animals and meaningful activities like cooking, taking attendance, or serving snacks provide the basis for learning activities.

6. Children work on projects and have long periods of time (at least an hour) to play and explore. Worksheets aren't used.

7. Children have an opportunity to play outside every day, and outdoor play is never omitted in favor of instructional time.

8. Teachers read books to children individually or in small groups throughout the day, not just at group story time.

9. The curriculum is matched to abilities of all children. Teachers recognize that children's different backgrounds and experiences mean they don't learn the same things at the same time in the same way.

10. Children and their parents look forward to school. Parents feel secure about sending their child to the program. Children are happy to attend; they do not cry regularly or complain of feeling sick.

Safety Issues

This is a place where your child will be cared for five days a week, five to six hours a day, and sometimes much longer. One of the most important things to pay attention to is how the program approaches safety issues. Health and safety should be their number-one priority. Following are some questions you'll want to have answered during your visit.

Is Food Prepared and Stored Safely?

The way food is handled is one of the most important issues in any child-care setting. Most centers provide lunch and a morning and/or afternoon snack. Some require parents to provide their child's lunch each day; some prepare lunch on location; others are catered from outside. If this school prepares lunch on location, the kitchen must pass government inspections several times a year.

Preschools must have large sinks, industrial-size refrigerators, dish-washers (for sterilizing), and garbage disposals. Each must be properly operating and cleaned daily. Use common sense when observing. For instance, if the school is not equipped with a dishwasher, the food should be served on plastic or on paper plates with disposable cups and utensils.

Catered food is usually freshly prepared the same day and should be delivered in proper containers and served soon after delivery. Every link in food handling could be a potential risk, so don't hesitate to find out how these transitions are handled.

With either onsite or catered meal options, the price is usually included in your tuition. Be sure to ask, because food costs could end up becoming an unwanted hidden expense.

What Is a Typical Menu Like?

Both the school and the caterer must follow guidelines for providing age-appropriate nutritional foods. Daily caloric intake and nutritional value needs vary from age to age. Many schools post their weekly and monthly lunch and snack menus. Ask to see them, if possible. Look for foods high in protein and vitamins.

Remember that many preschoolers can't eat enough in just three meals to get sufficient nutrients and calories, so they should have snacks between meals.

Although your child may need foods with some fats and sugar, there's no need for foods that are high in both. Some good snack foods include dry cereal with milk; whole-wheat crackers; peanut butter sandwiches; vegetable or fruit breads such as pumpkin or banana; animal crackers; fresh, dried, or canned fruit; fruit juice; yogurt; cheese and crackers; pretzels; and oatmeal cookies and milk.

Junk food is a real no-no. Candy bars and blue ice pops are not exactly the right way to start off your child's nutritional habits.

If your child has a special diet or suffers food allergies, good programs should readily accommodate his or her individual needs.

How Clean Is the Facility?

A good preschool is clean and safe; in fact, it has to be to meet most states' licensing requirements. It is vital that staff absolutely follow the school's hygiene procedures to protect children against contaminants.

Children play hard. Rooms must be cleaned and vacuumed daily. Kitchens and bathrooms must be cleaned daily—sometimes several times per day. Toys, tables, and any other items that children come in contact with have to be washed with a solution of bleach and water daily.

Pay attention to details such as what is being used to disinfect the diaper-changing areas, bathrooms, kitchen, and eating/playing areas. Most schools use a bleach and water solution as an effective and affordable disinfectant. Check to see which of these agents the preschool uses and if they are properly stored.

Make sure floors, walks, and the kitchen area are clean; food preparation areas are far from toilets; trash isn't left sitting unemptied; and the building is adequately heated, lit, and ventilated.

Watch especially to see how the school handles garbage. One of the strictest regulations for all child-care settings requires that all trash cans and diaper pails be covered.

What's the Hand-Washing Policy?

Ask about the preschool's hand-washing policy. If the director says there isn't one, watch out. Staff and teachers are required to wash their hands each time they use the lavatory or after coming in contact with children when feeding, changing diapers, or handling any body secretions. State licensing agencies set basic hygiene guidelines. Because this is a public health matter, preschools like many other public places must stick to them. It is possible that you have already seen posters with simple hygiene reminders like the ones reminding employees to properly wash their hands. You will find these in many public places such as restaurants or doctor's offices. Schools put them up, too.

During your visit, watch carefully to see if staffers use gloves and, if possible, observe hand-washing procedures. Most schools provide plastic gloves for serving food and surgical-type gloves for diaper changing.

But teachers aren't the only ones who should be washing their hands. Children should be actively taught how to wash their hands each time before eating and after using the restroom. Smart teachers post simple reminders (pictures or drawings of healthy habits) at children's eye level and reward them positively for being clean.

Are There Unpleasant Odors?

Although an occasional smelly diaper is expected in an infant room, be wary of the smell of urine in classrooms for older children.

Are Children Sharing Personal Items?

Children should not share sleeping mats or blankets or personal items such as toothbrushes, toothpaste, or combs and brushes. Personal possessions should be labeled, and soiled clothing should be sent home daily in appropriate wrapping (usually in plastic bags).

Some preschools have a laundry room complete with washer and dryer and a secure storage place for various cleaning agents such as bleach and detergents.

You should be concerned about hygiene because a child's immune system isn't fully developed at this age, so germs pose a more serious problem than they do to a healthy adult. Second, because of the rough-and-tumble way children play with each other, they are constantly exposed to a variety of germs that can easily spread from one child to another. The more precautions a school takes without being overly restrictive, the better.

Are Emergency Numbers Posted?

Look for posted emergency numbers during your visit. Emergency numbers should be posted next to telephones for immediate reference. Although everyone knows the 911 emergency number, not everyone has memorized the number for the local Poison Control Center—and in a case of poisoning, seconds count. Centers that have taken this into account are clearly better prepared should an accident occur.

Does the Facility Have a Fire Plan?

Remember the fire drills from grammar school? Well, you should expect the same sort of drill and degree of preparation in preschool. Fire code plans must be provided and posted throughout the center. Exit signs should be clearly marked, illuminated, and accessible.

Posters should show where you are in any given room and how to get out in the event of an emergency. Infant and toddler rooms should be close to the exit and on the ground floor. Exits should be clearly marked and exit routes free of clutter or other obstacles.

Children should be instructed what to do in the event of an emergency and must be familiar with the procedure. Teachers and staff should practice fire drills with students several times a month.

To work, a preschool fire safety program should involve both the children and their parents. Parents should also be given fire safety information and practice fire drills with their children at home.

Does the School Seem Aware of Important Safety Rules?

Let's face it—kids this age are curious, and they can get into trouble quite quickly. When you visit a potential preschool, scope out the room for uncovered outlets or exposed electrical wiring. Are cleaning products and other potentially toxic items kept safely locked out of reach?

Take a look at the overall school layout and how accessible these areas are to the children. For instance, the kitchen door, storage rooms, and adult restrooms should have childproof locks. Lack of procedures such as these may be warning signs of a center that is not up to the highest standards.

Make sure the preschool follows the basic rules of safety, too. Toys and play equipment should be in good repair, upstairs windows should have screens or bars, all medicines and other hazardous substances should be out of reach, and the outdoor play area should be level and secure.

Smoke detectors should be in place and working, radiators and heaters should be covered or otherwise protected, and a first-aid kit and fire extinguisher should be close at hand. The school should be secure as well so strangers can't just walk in off the street.

Is there space for active play and for quiet play? Is there a special place away from the busy activities for a sick or tired child to rest yet still be near the teacher? Can children reach the toilet and sink easily and safely?

Are Most of the Toys and Furniture Kid-Proof?

This is the question you might not need to ask—as a parent, you can probably tell right away. Make sure toys and furniture don't have sharp edges. Check to see if toys seem to be age appropriate.

If you have a younger child, it's especially important that toys are big enough that they can't be accidentally swallowed. Keep a sharp eye out for such items.

Carefully observe the toys that the children are given to play with. Toys that might promote violence or demonstrate undesirable stereotypes should never be used in preschools. You should be concerned if the preschool is filled with toy guns, spears, and swords, for example.

Each parent should address these issues individually as needed and not be afraid to raise concerns with staff and administrators. Good administrators will not be afraid to address your worries directly and forthrightly.

Be very careful to see if any furniture is finished with paint or varnish that a child could easily ingest after scratching or chewing. The reality is that kids often come into contact with such items by touching or licking the surfaces.

Are heavy pieces of furniture, such as storage shelves and bookcases, secure and stable so that they can't tip over?

Most good preschools will tell you what their school policy is on buying toys and children's furniture. Many order from companies that specialize in manufacturing items that meet only the strictest safety criteria.

Play Areas

Next, you'll want to take a good look at the play areas, both indoor and outdoor. Safe, up-to-date equipment and lots of space are imperative.

Does the Facility Have a Place for Exercise?

Look for a school with an outdoor play area. Children should have the chance to play outside every day—running, jumping, and skipping are good for them physically, mentally, and socially.

If you live in a city where it can be difficult for even the best preschools to have enough space for a safe outdoor play yard, make sure there is a spacious indoor area. Preschools should have at least 35 square feet of indoor space per child and 75 square feet per child outside.

If a preschool doesn't have a playground on the premises, the school might make use of a nearby park.

Whatever the situation, the bottom line is that children need physical activity as part of their daily routine and as part of their overall development. It's just as important for their development as educational puzzles, games, and toys.

Most schools provide children at least two hours of outdoor activities daily, weather permitting. Often, if the weather is bad, schools will reschedule their itinerary so that the children get at least some physical activities indoors.

What's the Playground Like?

Playgrounds can stimulate senses with different textures and contrasts in color. They can help develop dynamic balance by providing smaller children with small ramps or steps. They also may provide one of the first social experiences for some children. Good play areas offer children opportunities to play alone or with other children—but it's imperative that they're safe.

If the school does have a playground, you need to check it out thoroughly. Each year, more than 200,000 children are injured on America's playgrounds—that's 1 every $2^1/_2$ minutes. Determining how the staff feels about playground safety should be an important aspect of your visit to the preschool.

Ask to see the outdoor playground. Is the equipment age appropriate? Is there a fence around the entire play area, blocking access and visibility from the street?

Are the children adequately supervised? According to the National Program for Playground Safety, teachers should be actively observing all the children on the playground and should make sure shoes and clothing offer protection and don't have loose strings.

Nearly 70 percent of all playground injuries are related to falls. Check to see what type of shock-absorbing surfacing there is under play equipment. The type, depth, and area covered combine to create a safe play environment. Hard surfaces such as asphalt, blacktop, concrete, packed dirt, or grass are unacceptable. Preschools should use mulch or other wood products, rubber mats or tiles, pea gravel, sand, or rubber products.

Check to make sure the equipment is anchored safely in the ground, all equipment pieces are in good working order, S hooks on swings are entirely closed, bolts are not protruding, and there are no exposed cement footings anchoring the equipment to the ground. Equipment should be well maintained and appropriate for the age of the children. There should be no spaces between 3½ inches to 9 inches in which a child's head or body could get stuck.

Appropriate play areas for children ages two to five could include areas to crawl, low platforms with multiple access (such as ramps and ladders), ramps with pieces attached for grasping, low tables for sand or water, tricycle paths, flexible spring rockers, covered sand areas, shorter slides (usually no taller than four feet), activity panels, swings, crawl tunnels, and playhouses.

The playground should allow younger children to easily manipulate items, explore spaces, and begin to interact with others. Equipment such as appropriately sized slides and swings encourage children to experiment.

Appropriately designed playgrounds allow younger children to explore new methods of playing and to take reasonable risks. Parents can help nurture this development by observing, supervising, and complimenting, but not directly interfering unless there is a safety problem.

What's the Park Like?

If the children don't have a playground but instead visit a nearby park, be sure to check this out, too. Note how far the area is from the school. Do children have to walk very far to get there? How many streets do they have to cross? Are there busy intersections?

Very small children can ride in large strollers that accommodate up to eight kids—and have been known to attract the attention of more than a few adults with comments of how cute they look together! Typically, older children are taught to hold hands as they walk to the park, or they grab onto a rope that keeps all the children in line.

Note the condition of the park. Is it well kept and litter free? How many other people use the park during the day? Are there any obvious security concerns? Have there ever been any incidents in the park you should know about? How many teachers and staff accompany the children on their daily trip? Do they carry cellular telephones? Is this the kind of place you would bring your child on your own?

What Kind of Physical Activities Are Provided?

The school's activities should promote both group and individual play. Children need to be actively engaged in running, skipping, climbing, hopping, and jumping to ensure the appropriate development of their gross motor skills.

Equipment and games that encourage this development should be age and size appropriate, but here's what to look for:

- Jump ropes
- Balls
- Bicycles
- Hoops
- Scooters
- Jungle-gym

Group activities should encourage children to play cooperatively in teams, but competition should be discouraged at this early age. All violent games should be strictly prohibited.

Imitating violent figures or acting out violent scenes from television or movies should be strongly discouraged. Someone will inevitably get hurt, and that's not the kind of activity you should be paying a preschool for.

Do the teachers respect the children's rights to engage in activities by themselves and with other children? Is the space arranged so children can freely select materials according to their own interests and return them when they have finished?

Do you hear adults praising and encouraging children? Do the children seem to be enjoying the activities? Is the program well stocked with equipment and supplies such as blocks, books, games, toys, and creative art materials?

Does the Staff Seem Aware of Health Issues? Do Teachers Know CPR?

Preschools require that all teachers and staff be in good health and free of any communicable diseases. In addition, teachers and staff members should be required to pass yearly health exams and should also be required to successfully pass exams for cardiopulmonary resuscitation (CPR) and first aid.

The Second Visit ...

If what you've seen and heard on your first visit pleases you, arrange a second visit so you can bring along your child. Bring your spouse along if you toured the school alone the first time. This second visit is a good time to discuss with the director any questions you may still have.

On the second visit, pay attention to the activities and interactions of the teachers and children. Don't worry if your child hesitates about joining in. This is a new experience, and preschool is still several months away. Your child will develop and mature during those months.

Bring Questions

Although you may already have some brochures from each school, they probably won't tell you everything you need to know. Information may be outdated or slanted to show only the school's best profile with boilerplate language that glosses over important details. Many will tell you about "qualified personnel," "low student-teacher ratios," and "a dedication to students' welfare." But do they really offer these? As a parent and a consumer, you have every right to demand quality for your money.

That's why it's especially important that you come prepared with the right questions in hand on your return visit. Don't be afraid to show up with a notepad and a pen. Far from being offended, the better schools you visit will likely be impressed by your thoroughness and attention to detail. Jot notes down when you need to.

This will also help you later when you sit down to go over all the information you've assembled on candidate schools—an especially useful trick if you're planning on visiting quite a few. After a few visits, if you don't take good notes, everything starts to blend together into one big frenetic blur of children and schools.

In the Next Chapter

You've learned how to check out the quality of the preschool environment. In the next chapter, we'll discuss everything you should know about a good preschool curriculum.

Chapter 6

The Preschool Curriculum:
Learning from A to Z

Behind every successful preschool program you will find a well-planned curriculum. Even though you might not immediately know whether you're getting what you and your child were promised in the brochure, you can feel more confident about assessing what you see in a preschool after familiarizing yourself with the basics of preschool learning. Even though preschool programs vary, you should be able to recognize some common curriculum guidelines all successful preschools follow.

During the 1980s, many early childhood programs concentrated on teaching basic academic skills because experts believed there was a need to prepare preschoolers for what they would face in kindergarten and first grade. Unfortunately, this approach developed into a tendency to rush children and push them too fast to begin formal learning. Children who are pushed to achieve beyond their developmental abilities become anxious and overstressed. And stressing academic skills over creative ability can result in stifling talents and other gifts.

Over the past few years, there has been a shift toward providing more child-initiated activities that offer children opportunities to directly experience and manipulate new ideas and objects.

Today, high-quality early childhood programs do much more than simply teach children their colors, numbers, letters, and shapes. Good programs help children learn *how to learn* and to question why and discover alternative answers.

Discovering the Curriculum

You can expect most preschools to offer you a curriculum handbook and/ or videotape. This material should be a pretty good guide to the school's outlook on preschool education and overall childhood development. The statements found in these booklets and videos must follow the developmental guidelines established by your state's Department of Education, in collaboration with local boards of education.

Many schools will go into detail about these guidelines, explaining the emphasis of their program and what makes their school unique. This can be a good way for you to begin asking yourself what will really work for you and your child. You should carefully read all the material the school provides, and don't be afraid to ask questions about it. Generally, a curriculum handbook should cover all aspects of a child's learning: social-emotional development, language, creative arts, math and science, social studies, and health and physical development. Information on classroom environment and individual child assessment plans should also be included.

It's just about impossible to keep a young child from learning; providing essentials such as stimulating materials, experiences and learning opportunities, support, and encouragement is the best way to help children develop their full potential. Your child will do the rest as the developmental level expands.

Lesson Plans

Each week, the teacher's lesson plan should contain the following elements:

- Language arts: In-depth language development activities on a daily basis.
- Math skills: Math skills development activities should be included daily.
- Science: Science experiments, including cooking, should occur once a week.
- Physical activities: Daily exercise is essential for overall development.
- Arts and crafts: Art activities should be included daily.

All of these categories may by nature include or be related to social-emotional development and social studies. While engaging in many different activities, children learn about themselves and others, learn to cooperate, learn languages, and so on. Each category may be a part of a specific theme. For example, while children discuss the recyclable items they have collected (**social studies; ecology**), they plan an **art** or a **science** project they may use them for. In the end, children's art objects may be used for an exhibition in the local children's hospital (**social studies; community awareness**).

Outdoor Play

The outdoor play area should include the following materials:

- Riding toys
- At least two large climbing structures in good condition that follow current safety standards
- Soft materials (such as mulch or shredded tires) under climbing structures, slides, swings, and other "landing" areas
- Slides appropriate to the children's height and age
- A large sandbox and digging toys (sandbox should be covered at night)

- Large building materials such as waffle blocks
- Tunnels, playhouses, and other structures to climb in and through
- Jump ropes, sidewalk chalk, and other additional materials.

Swings: A Safety Note

Although swings are safe for use with older groups of children, they can pose a hazard to mixed-age groups such as mixed two-, three-, and four-year-olds. Two-year-olds are not well aware of their surroundings and are often hurt by falling off or getting hit by swings. Also, younger twos and threes are not as coordinated as fours and fives and do not hold on to the swings properly. If the school has swings, they should be adapted for all ages (height, safety belts, or closed seats, etc.). Also, ask teachers how they monitor for safety.

What you don't want to see in a preschool is a lot of TV watching; in fact, you might want to question why children in preschool are watching TV at all. Research has proven that time in excess of one hour per day in front of the television lessens a child's level of motivation to learn independently. If TV watching is a part of the curriculum, content should be limited to educational, musical, and interactive programs. For this age group, watching time should not exceed one hour per week.

Computers are present in many classrooms for fours and fives. As long as the software is age appropriate, computers can be excellent tools for strengthening skills like hand and eye coordination, thinking, and problem-solving. They are often incorporated in the curriculum but might be used for fun individually and can be shared by a few children at the same time. While playing a computer game together, children learn to cooperate and enjoy the results of team playing.

Teaching Methods

When it comes to teaching, there is no "best" method. In general, you'd want to see an approach that avoids anything that might discourage the learning process. For example, when a child gives a wrong answer, teachers should avoid the words "no," "wrong," or "that's not right." Instead, the child should be encouraged to try again—or the teacher may simply pause until the child tries again to come up with a different answer.

In the year before kindergarten, it may be possible for your child to learn to count and to learn letter names and some letter sounds, but this isn't really what's important in kindergarten readiness. There are much more important things to learn during the preschool years to build a strong foundation for future school success. In a good preschool, only brief periods should be spent on academic subjects such as letters, numbers, and colors—with lots of activity in between.

Children will find it relatively easy to learn early reading and number skills in kindergarten and first grade if they have a rich knowledge base, good language skills, listening comprehension and attention management skills, and a positive attitude toward learning and toward themselves as learners.

Preschoolers learn best when they are interested in hands-on activities, when they have readily available adult support, and when activities are related to what they already know.

When you see children playing with blocks, they are really learning math concepts such as long, short, heavy, light, counting, problem-solving (as they try to create with blocks), predicting (as they create roadways for racing cars), and shapes.

They are learning social skills as they make building-block towers and castles and parking garages with other children.

Language development occurs as they talk with one another and as an astute teacher asks questions and makes comments to expand their ideas.

They learn intellectual skills such as prereading and writing as they create signs for the "downtown" area they have created or as the teacher reads a story about community helpers who work in a city.

In each "center" of the classroom, including drama, blocks, table toys, art, library, music, sensory, and science areas, children are learning many educational concepts in a manner that is meaningful to them.

Following are some examples of widely accepted curriculum guidelines nationwide, based on research and studies in early childhood education, that foster these and other skills and help children learn how to learn.

Social-Emotional Development

General Expectations

During the preschool years, children should ...

- Develop self-awareness and interpersonal communication skills.
- Develop self-esteem, self-confidence, and independence.
- Build relationships with peers through play. They should learn about feelings, interests, and needs of others.
- Learn problem-solving skills.
- Learn and demonstrate positive behavior. They should be able to express their own feelings in an appropriate manner.

One of the most challenging parts of growing up is being able to determine how you fit in with the rest of the world. Experts believe that the quality of a child's social and emotional development is the most reliable predictor of school performance and overall success in life.

If children feel good about themselves and are comfortable in familiar surroundings, chances are they will be able to positively express their feelings, needs, and observations. They will also communicate with peers in an acceptable way, have a better sense of their role in the group, and better understand the needs and feelings of others.

They learn to feel good about themselves in welcoming, safe, and predictable environments, where the rules are consistent, materials are accessible, and teachers are steady, friendly, and sensitive to the children's needs and differences.

Good programs will arrange available spaces and plan and implement activities that promote positive social interaction while also allowing space for individuality and self-expression. Children should be able either to play alone or with their peers, as they wish. They should be able to play cooperatively in small groups and follow group rules such as taking turns, sharing, giving and receiving, articulating wants and needs, and so on.

They should be encouraged to make choices and explore their senses with a variety of materials. For instance, clay molding and water play are great stress relievers. Listening to a story on tape encourages them to use their imagination while improving listening skills and concentration.

Children in preschool should be able to identify problems and conflicts and practice problem-solving through conversations, negotiations, and compromise. They should be able to discuss their own daily experiences, look at appropriate books, watch videos with themes children can relate to, and so on.

They should be learning to set their own limits, identify their own feelings, and understand the feelings of others. They should be able to communicate feelings and thoughts with adults and peers equally.

Independence should be encouraged during the preschool years. At this age, children should learn some basic self-help skills, such as feeding and dressing themselves, and maintaining basic hygiene like hand washing and tooth brushing. They should be able to take care of their toilet needs independently and know how to use a tissue or handkerchief.

Learning how to predict outcomes, reason, empathize, show affection, participate in a group, and be helpful are just some of the challenges children must go through on their path to a healthy adjustment.

Creative Arts

General Expectations

During the preschool years, children should ...

- Develop appreciation for visual art, music, and visual self-expression.
- Be able to express themselves through dramatic play.
- Explore their tactile and visual senses through use of a variety of art materials.
- Recognize and name primary colors.
- Recognize shapes, including circles and rectangles.
- Match shapes or objects based on shape.

One of the most comfortable ways for children to express themselves is through art. In good preschools, creative arts are incorporated into all curriculum areas. In a good program, you should see art activities explored daily—painting one day, glue and glitter the next.

If used in appropriate ways, art can be a very important part of learning. It promotes exploration, verbal, and nonverbal expression, and it's a good tool for introducing and presenting many other subjects.

Children should be exposed to varieties of art expressions, including music, painting, and theater. They should experience hands-on activities by using a variety of materials.

Not only is art a fun activity that encourages creativity, but it also allows children to develop fine motor muscles as they manipulate materials. For example, holding a marker is one of the first steps toward learning how to write.

Materials that develop fine motor skills and coordination for very young children include crayons, paper, blunt scissors, glue, simple puzzles, and construction-type materials such as Legos. The items should be small enough to provide a challenge and large enough to allow the child to use them successfully (and too big to get stuck in the nose, ear, or throat). Paper, glue, paint, glitter, buttons, and wooden beads are some of the materials children love using.

Even though children enjoy seeing the finished art product, they should be encouraged to focus on the *process* of creating. As children experiment with various artistic media, they learn about shapes and colors and experience textures.

Painting and music can be very soothing and can help children this age relax. Dancing gives children the opportunity to learn about their bodies, spatial relations, and rhythm. Dramatic play can include story-telling, puppets, and singing. Children should participate in role-playing and use their imagination and props as well as imitate actions and sounds.

Watching performances and visiting museums and galleries are fun ways of learning about the world of art and its diversity and should be a part of the curriculum in every preschool.

Health and Physical Development

General Expectations

In preschool, children should ...

- Develop appropriate hygiene and nutritional habits.
- Develop coordination, strength, and balance through gross motor activities.
- Develop fine motor coordination through appropriate activities.

The role of the preschool in promoting physical development is to provide healthful and nourishing meals and snacks, adequate rest or nap periods, and developmentally appropriate physical activities involving different kinds of equipment and materials.

When considering the strength of a program in physical development, you want to look for a variety of physical equipment for different ages, adequate space for supervised physical play inside and out, scheduled free play time, and simple structured activities both inside and out.

Children can work on gross motor development, balance, coordination, and strength during free play time as well as during simple, structured activities. The ideal environment will include a large, secure, and supervised outdoor play area with objects such as wagons, bikes, boxes, large balls, and climbing gyms.

As children mature and gain in coordination, strength, and endurance, periods of free play interspersed with short periods of more organized activities appeal to them. Free play time needs to be scheduled at times that do not overlap with use of the same areas by older, larger children.

Physical fitness for preschool children should also include some lessons in hygiene and nutrition. Children should be encouraged to taste healthful foods. Although a child's nutritional habits largely depend on cultural background and upbringing, teachers should be prepared to help children choose what's best for them and help them understand the importance of good nutrition. They should closely work with families and be sensitive to cultural differences. Children should also practice using utensils and serving themselves and others.

At the same time, children should be taught to maintain basic hygiene, such as using toilets, properly washing hands, cleaning after themselves, and so on. For example, learning about germs and how they spread is very important in a preschool setting. It can also help prevent illness outbreaks.

Setting a good example by cleaning tables and maintaining an orderly classroom are good ways to teach children about health, and you should see this happening in a good preschool.

Playing outdoors has always been a favorite children's activity. Good preschools should aim to spend *at least* one hour a day at the playground or in the park, weather permitting.

Every preschool should have some kind of physical activity outlet, whether it's an attached playground, nearby park, or even an indoor gymnasium. Preschool children need to spend time on gross motor activities like running, skipping, pushing and pulling toys, riding tricycles, and tossing and kicking balls. They also enjoy climbing, crawling, jumping, and rolling and should be encouraged to exercise daily—always under staff supervision.

Teachers should be well aware of the benefits of good daily exercise for children. If outdoor facilities aren't available or the weather is poor, teachers should spend some time on active play indoors such as having a marching band or dancing.

As children engage in these activities, they learn about their bodies, physical limits, and coordination. When children participate in group games, they practice taking turns and cooperating. They think and take initiative.

Young children need small motor development as well. By age three or four, a child should be able to make vertical, horizontal, and circular strokes with a pencil or crayon and turn a book's pages one at a time. They should be able to complete simple puzzles, draw and color beyond a simple scribble, and control the pencil and crayon well. They should be able to cut simple shapes and handle scissors well.

Engaging preschoolers in manual activities throughout the day contributes to the development of their eye-hand coordination. For instance, modeling clay, puzzles, blocks, and lacing are excellent ways of preparing little fingers for even more precise tasks later on. In addition, children should participate in finger plays and songs and folding and tearing paper.

Language Development

General Expectations
During the preschool years, children should ...

- Be exposed to oral and written language, including foreign languages.
- Be encouraged to tell stories, listen, and communicate with others.
- Be engaged in activities promoting reading and writing skills.
- Have the opportunity to learn about other ways of communicating, such as using sign language.

Most important language development occurs during the early childhood years. By age two, most children can tell you their names and the names of common objects and can use a vocabulary of about 50 words. They can speak in three- or four-word sentences and even hold a brief conversation.

By age three, many children can recognize several letters, use pronouns, and understand plurals. By the time they are four, they can speak clearly enough for anyone to understand them, and they can tell a story. Some children are also able to write letters of the alphabet at this age.

Because a child's social and academic future will depend on the level of literacy they achieve, it's extremely important to provide young children with a variety of language and literacy experiences as early as possible. Every preschool teacher should introduce language arts to preschool children in ways that will enable children to develop their full literacy potential.

"Literacy" consists of speaking, listening, reading, writing, and viewing visual information. Children should be engaged in activities promoting all these components.

In addition, children should be exposed to materials that represent the child's own and others' languages as much as possible. Some inclusive programs, for instance, provide language and literacy experiences for children of different cultural backgrounds. The purpose is to strengthen first language capabilities and create a good base for learning English.

They should be exposed to a discussion of position and direction, understanding up and down, in and out, front and back, over and under, top and bottom, beside and next to, hot and cold, and fast and slow.

Listening

At the very least, preschool children should be able to follow simple oral directions, answer questions, and identify sounds in the environment. They should listen to short stories both read and narrated. They should hear rhymes and poems in their own and other languages and hear language spoken by different adults. They should be able to repeat a sequence of sounds or a sequence of orally given numbers and should be able to retell simple stories in sequence.

Speaking

Children should be encouraged to communicate in verbal and nonverbal language. They should ask questions, use words to express feelings or make requests, describe their own experiences, make connections, and interact with peers and adults. They should participate in storytelling, singing, role-playing, and finger playing; use puppets or other props to tell and retell stories; and so on.

Reading

Children in preschool are not "taught" to read, but that doesn't mean books aren't important at this age. The first signs of print awareness begin with books. Children should handle books, turn the pages, pretend to read, verbally label objects and characters, and make comments on what they see. Books in a typical preschool classroom should reflect the cultural diversity and variety of topics children this age can relate to. (For a full list of excellent books for preschool-age children, see Appendix E.)

Adults are always the best role models for children, especially in the classroom, so children should see teachers reading good literature.

Teachers should encourage further print awareness by labeling objects throughout the classroom and by displaying print at a child's eye level. For instance, teachers should print a child's name next to the appropriate coat hanger or cubby and should label all crafts. Alphabet posters are a good way of decorating the classroom.

Teachers should help children identify print in the local environment and point out different purposes of written language. For example, while walking outdoors, children can be asked to look for specific store signs. Activities like "reading" a magazine or a grocery list are good tools for promoting reading readiness.

Children this age should be able to remember an object from a given picture and understand what a letter is. They should be able to recognize some nursery rhymes, identify the parts of the body, and recognize common farm and zoo animals. They should be able to identify other children by name, tell the meaning of simple words, and complete an incomplete sentence with the proper word.

They should use left-to-right progression, be able to answer questions about a short story, tell the meaning of words heard in story, and look at pictures and tell a story.

Writing

Children enjoy experimenting with writing and drawing tools such as pencils, crayons, markers, chalk, rubber stamps, and computers. They are intrigued by different writing surfaces and love scribbling on all kinds of paper, wood, and chalkboard.

They should draw, imitate writing, use all types of letterforms for tracing, and watch adults while recording dictated stories and making charts. Activities like these will help them comprehend the written language and its purpose. They should be able to identify their own first name on a written page and be able to print it.

Other Language Uses

Each preschooler should learn about other ways of communicating such as sign language and experience language through different media such as video and audio messages or interactive software, and symbols in the environment, such as traffic or directional signs.

Mathematics

General Expectations

During the preschool years, children should ...

- Experience math problem-solving skills through hands-on activities.
- Connect mathematical ideas with real-life experiences and explore numeration, geometrical shapes, and measurement concepts.
- Understand the concept of size, such as big and little, long and short.
- Match shapes or objects based on size.
- Count orally through 10.
- Understand concepts like empty and full, more and less.

Just like everything else in a good preschool program, mathematics should be presented to children in a meaningful context. Children this age learn best if they are allowed to experience math in everyday life. By age three, many children can recognize several numbers.

You can expect to see mathematics being introduced every day via hands-on activities with a variety of tools and props, real-life situations, and discussions. These activities are usually initiated by the child during play, but teachers should be ready with open-ended questions. The best learning happens when children enjoy the activity. They will understand better if the math concepts are presented to them as part of their everyday routine.

Some of the typical appropriate practices in teaching basic math concepts include the following:

- Sorting, matching, and classifying: sorting shells, leaves or nuts, pattern picture cards, or matching mittens by shape, size, color, or pattern
- Communicating experiences: songs and finger-plays, describing how they build with blocks, drawing
- Visual/verbal number representations: counting on fingers, setting tables for snacks, counting objects, etc
- Sequential and spatial relations: learning concepts of first and last, behind, next, up and down, putting puzzles together, etc
- Money and its value: grocery store play, running a lemonade stand, visiting a bank, piggy banks
- Measuring, estimating, and differentiating: using measuring spoons and cups while cooking, building tall and short block towers, guessing how many steps there are on the way to the park, experiencing heavy and light, etc.
- Graphic representations: daily discussions with calendars, weather charts, and growth charts children have helped create, etc.

Science

General Expectations

During the preschool years, children should ...

- Discover and explore their five senses and their uses.
- Explore nature and through appropriate activities gain necessary skills to relate to the environment.
- Be able to make simple predictions in age-appropriate experiments.

Almost all children are born "scientists" with boundless curiosity and a zest for exploration. The first step in discovery of the surrounding world is through their five senses. Children learn to use all their senses—sight, touch, sound, smell, and taste—at an early age. The purpose of science education in preschool is to preserve and further develop this natural sense of wonder.

The best learning at the preschool age happens during play, which is a primary step in every child's cognitive development. It enables them to process information and apply their own experiences. As they interact with the living world and come in contact with various materials, children use their senses and learn skills that help them comprehend the basic scientific principles.

Knowledgeable teachers understand the importance of "teachable moments" and will take clues from children, ask open-ended questions, and allow children to experiment, investigate, and come to their own con-clusions through trial and error.

Through a variety of simple experiments children should ...

- Learn about their senses.
- Predict and observe the outcomes of simple experiments such as mix-ing colors or cooking.
- Learn about the natural world, life cycles, habitats, and differences between the living and the nonliving world (such as the fact that peo-ple and animals need water, plants come from seeds, animal homes, and so on).
- Explore the earth's properties by observing weather and season changes; experimenting with water, soil, and magnets; and so on.
- Be familiar with the solar system, such as being able to name the planets, know facts about the sun and moon, and how they affect the living on earth.
- Participate in caring for the environment by cleaning up and recy-cling and caring for belongings and properties.

Social Studies

General Expectations

During the preschool years, children should ...

- Develop self-awareness and interpersonal communication skills.
- Learn concepts of family and family traditions.
- Learn about their own and other cultures.
- Develop awareness of their communities.
- Explore the concepts of basic economic processes.
- Be aware of environmental issues.

With the first signs of self-awareness, children also become curious about the way the world around them works. Preschoolers readily absorb what surrounds them and start realizing that there is a place for them in their families, in the classroom, and in their community.

The first steps, such as communicating with adults and peers and learning about independence and a sense of belonging, are tremendously important. Children should be capable of exhibiting positive individual and group behaviors.

Establishing and following rules while being able to resolve conflicts in socially acceptable ways are great skills young ones should start learning at this age. Demonstrating an appreciation for individual differences and similarities leads to a healthy self-concept and better overall adjustment later on.

Helping children understand their own role in the family, identify family members, and develop awareness of their own and other cultures is essential. Every teacher knows that children enjoy celebrations and holidays and love participating in observing traditions. One of the most rewarding ways in which any culture can be introduced is through language. It is proven that young children grasp maternal as well as foreign languages easily and learn fast.

Children should taste different foods, listen to international music, and be exposed to many aspects of our diverse society along with customs and traditions from all over the world.

While walking around the neighborhood, children become aware of the basic community structure as seen in community services and different occupations. They should visit workplaces and talk to workers about their jobs.

When visiting stores and restaurants, children become aware of basic daily economics, such as buying and selling. They should reenact their experiences in the classroom by manufacturing different products. For example, they could make bead jewelry, bake cookies, "record" (with a teacher) their own daily news, and play "store."

Children this age are capable of understanding basic environmental principles. They should learn what causes pollution and what they can do to help their communities. They should learn about preservation and recycling. For example, many materials, such as cardboard boxes, plastic bottles, fabric scraps, and old stationery, can be recycled and used in the classroom for different projects.

All the areas of development we've covered in this chapter are equally important. However, children may not engage in all activities provided, and all good programs will provide many opportunities for all interests. Teachers must be aware that children develop at different rates. The balance between what children can do and what the curriculum offers is the key to success. Remember that forcing children to do things will only increase the risk of rejection. Good preschools will want good results of their teaching, and they will do everything to prevent negative experiences for children.

In the Next Chapter

Now that you've learned what to expect in a good preschool curriculum, in the next chapter we'll discuss the qualifications you should look for in a good preschool teacher.

Chapter 7

Who's Teaching Your Child?

The best-equipped preschool in the world is not a good choice if the teachers running the program aren't top-notch. Ideally, you and your child's preschool teacher will work as a team dedicated to making your child's first school years happy and productive.

Teachers should be responsible, enthusiastic, and well prepared, sharing your philosophies on key child-rearing issues such as sleep, discipline, and nutrition. Good teachers will ask detailed questions about your child's health and care requirements to help determine whether their preschool is right for you.

Basic Teacher Requirements

Preschool teachers should be well educated, with at least two years of college, a background in early childhood development (though many states don't require this), and CPR and other emergency training. Because most preschool teachers are trained in early childhood education, they know what to expect from your child developmentally.

Studies have consistently found that it's the teacher who makes a difference in whether or not children profit from preschool activities. It's the teacher who plans the activities, interacts with children, and encourages the child's intellectual and social development. This is why the lead teachers, assistants, and aides in a preschool program should have training in early childhood education and child development. Although the lead teachers might have the most expertise, do not dismiss the importance of experience and personality as well. The co-teaching staff might have a little less background in this field, but oftentimes these dedicated people are truly valuable additions to the teaching team. They might have other related experiences and education such as nursing, art, or social studies. Some of them have retired from their previous positions and make excellent aids.

Student/Teacher Ratio

Make sure the preschool has plenty of staff so your child will get the attention and care he needs. According to the National Association for the Education of Young Children (NAEYC), a preschool should have 1 teacher for every 10 children. (Even that number is high; a ratio of 1:8 or 1:9 is better for 4- and 5-year-olds; 3-year-olds do best with 1 teacher for every 7 children.)

Children benefit from interacting with their peers, but in some preschools, emphasis on groups can overshadow the individual attention kids need and crave. This is a particular risk if the preschool doesn't follow the NAEYC's recommended teacher-child ratio.

Note that preschools aren't *required* to follow NAEYC's recommendations, so ask what each school's teacher-child ratio is and decide whether that's okay for your child. A good preschool will keep groups of children small no matter how many teachers they have to encourage interaction and development.

Evaluating the Preschool Director

Although the quality of your child's teacher is of vital importance, the preschool director sets the tone for the entire school.

The director is responsible for teachers and students, food and facilities, materials, and the curriculum. This busy manager keeps track of quality review reports for various local and state agencies and hires, trains, and evaluates the teachers. This is the person who resolves conflicts among teachers as well as disputes between parents and staff members. Other duties include recruiting new teachers and students, reviewing curricular materials, and planning or writing the center newsletter and other materials.

The director must substitute teach when a staff member is absent and arrange care or pick-up for an injured or sick child. Parents have to assess the directors of their children's current or possible future child-care programs. They can do this only by asking the right questions—an approach that is fair and perfectly appropriate.

There are no unbreakable rules about when to ask the questions below. You might toss out some questions at the first meeting or the second. You could do it while touring the facility or when meeting the administrator in the front office. Use your best judgment.

However, you should make sure that as many questions as possible are answered by the facility's director or assistant director. This is the person who is responsible for maintaining the school, and you aren't likely to get all the information you need by randomly asking teachers. The director is the person you'll need to consult in the event of a problem at the school you eventually choose.

How well the questions are answered can give you a good idea of how dedicated directors are and how seriously they feel about the success of their center. It's easy to spot fake enthusiasm if you probe deeply enough. Real dedication to children, however, will shine through. Believe me, you'll know.

The following questions are good indicators of the professional strength and competence of a preschool director and will help you assess the quality of a preschool program.

How Long Have You Served in This Position?

What other supervisory positions have you held in preschool programs? Were you a teacher in this or a similar preschool facility before becoming the director? If so, how do you describe yourself as a teacher?

The longer they've served in the position, the better. It takes time and effort to create a good environment for children and teachers. Experience counts, but the quality of the program will depend greatly on the director. Many people who manage preschools are truly interested in children's welfare and very enthusiastic about their profession. Really good directors will give you a lot of details about how things are done in their centers.

What Are Your Occupancy Rates?

If the preschool has a good reputation in the community, the classes will likely be at near-capacity compared to similar ones in the community.

What Is the Return Rate?

What percentage of families return to the center year after year? What percentage of families subsequently enroll other children?

Good programs usually serve generations of families. If about 75 percent of siblings come back, chances are that this school's reputation is good. Also, ask if the school has a waiting list.

How Well Do Staff Members Work Together?

When there are staff conflicts, how does the director manage the issues? Is there a conflict-resolution plan for the center? A center that deals well with inevitable conflicts among staff will be a more pleasant place to work and lead to a less-stressful environment for both teachers and students.

What Are Your Feelings About Accreditation?

If the school is not accredited, do you have plans for achieving accreditation?

Of course, many perfectly good preschools do not have accreditation, but it's always good to hear that a school is willing to go an extra mile.

What Is Your Educational Philosophy?

Is the director's description consistent with what you observe at the center? Look for concrete examples of the director's philosophy in classroom activities. For example, if the center's philosophy emphasizes creativity and plays down the use of rote learning and workbooks but you see children busily filling out page after page of mimeographed worksheets, there's a conflict between philosophy and reality.

Describe the Preschool's Curriculum

What are daily examples of curriculum activities that make it clear what the children are learning?

What's Your Discipline Policy?

Spanking is obviously not a choice. Young children usually act in inappropriate ways when their wants or needs aren't being met. A good teacher will help children develop the ability to express those wants and needs appropriately by ...

- Teaching them to express their emotions.
- Helping them solve problems by making choices.
- Redirecting children to areas of play where they can be successful.
- Establishing rules and teaching children the process for following those rules.

Discipline should be seen as a positive way of teaching children how to manage their own behavior. The preschool's brochure should describe their behavior guidance perspective. Read it carefully and ask questions.

How Often Do You Communicate with Parents?

You should hear all about the news of the preschool on a regular basis: upcoming parenting workshops, volunteer needs, new books and toys, parent resources, new teachers and teacher assistants, your child's development.

Ask the director if you should expect notes to be posted on a bulletin board or newsletters to be sent home. Is there a parent resource room or bulletin board readily visible?

Is the Preschool Sensitive to the Cultural and Language Needs of Parents and Children?

Posters and family pictures on the walls and shelves should reflect the multicultural society of the United States. Do you see books about minority children representative of children living in the United States?

What Resources Are Available to Teachers, Children, and Parents?

Are there computers in any of the classrooms? Is there a variety of well-maintained books and toys available?

Many schools subscribe to publications that deal with children and parenting issues and have their own library with all related literature. Parents and teachers are welcome to borrow the material such as books, videos, and magazines.

Does the Center Have Business and Social Service Partners in the Community?

Are there local social service organizations that offer workshops in the preschool facility, or is the program linked to other services or local businesses?

A program that offers lots of links to community services can be a valuable resource to parents. This also means that a center is dedicated to constant improvement in all areas, such as health and safety, and provides information about financial and other help to the families in need. Many parents are not aware of such opportunities, and good preschools understand the benefits of helping children and their families.

Do Staff Members Participate in Professional Workshops?

Do the director and staff attend workshops and in-services that keep them abreast of current trends in the field?

It is essential for any good preschool program to keep improving its services. Teaching, for instance, is a highly stressful profession. Periodic workshops and lectures on how to manage stress or improve the communication between parents and teachers and among staff help a lot.

What Are the Staff Benefits?

Look for a preschool with good staff benefits. Preschools that treat their employees well and offer them good benefits such as vacation time, health insurance, and an education allowance, for example, are more likely to retain their teachers for many years.

A preschool with good staff benefits is likely to have less teacher turnover, which means consistent care for your child.

What Is the Teacher Turnover Rate?

How stable is the child-care staff? Low turnover is the key to ensuring consistent, stable care for your child. If all the teachers in the school have only been there a year or two, or they seem overwhelmed and inexperienced, keep looking.

High turnover rates could mean that the school is not a very pleasant working environment for teachers—and if teachers aren't happy there, odds are the children won't be either. Consistency is important in preschool. Will your child often be faced with a new caregiver in his classroom? He or she will learn less if there is a steady parade of teachers.

How Do You Evaluate Your Staff?

When evaluating the staff and the program, what quality indicators do you emphasize and why?

The director and other managing staff, such as assistant directors and program coordinators (who can also be lead teachers), are in charge of observing the staff performance periodically and on a daily basis. The forms and checklists they use during observations will be confidential and the director will use them for formal evaluations. These evaluations usually take place once or twice a year. This helps the staff improve their teaching methods, classroom management, and teamwork.

How Much Experience Do Your Teachers Have?

Clearly, you'll want to have teachers with years of teaching experience, but this isn't always possible. Economic realities today mean that many teachers are relatively young or just out of school (20 to 25 years old).

You'll also find preschool teachers at the other end of the age spectrum, especially if they are returning to teaching after retirement. Low pay at most preschools makes it very hard to keep qualified young professionals willing to work at stress-filled jobs requiring time and dedication.

The most important point, however, is not necessarily age, but how long the staff has worked together as a team. A preschool may have a pool of extremely talented young people individually, but if they don't work together as a team, the whole school suffers.

What Are Your Hiring Policies?

Ask how the school recruits and selects staff. Find out how thoroughly they check references, background checks, and previous employment history. Many places are in desperate need for staff and usually settle for less, especially when hiring the assistant teachers and aids.

Do the Teachers Have Degrees in Early Childhood Education?

The better preschools will have many teachers and administrators with degrees in early childhood education. Many colleges and universities offer this specialty both at the undergraduate and graduate levels. Some schools require their primary teachers to have attained at least one of these degrees, if not both, although experience is almost always a key factor in hiring.

Assistants and other aides will more likely have Associate's degrees or a high school diploma, but they should have successfully completed a certification program.

This does not mean that all the better teachers have degrees in early childhood education. It's entirely possible to find bright, motivated, and successful teachers with degrees in related fields such as psychology, sociology, social work, art, and so on. Some individuals who don't have advanced degrees have entered the field equipped with talent, enthusiasm, and creativity.

Would You Mind If I Spoke to the Teachers?

Speaking directly with teachers gives you an excellent opportunity to meet educators on their home turf before committing to a particular school. The real proof of quality is not always a glossy pamphlet or a diploma hanging on the wall, but the actual teaching going on inside the class-room.

Although most schools really aren't under an obligation to allow you to talk to their teachers, many of the better ones will likely not object. Bear in mind, however, that teachers are extremely busy. You'll have to accommodate your schedule to theirs, not vice versa.

If the school doesn't object, ask to see teachers who will be instructing at your child's age level. This not only gives you the chance to find out a little more about someone who could likely be your child's teacher, but it also gives you a chance to see whether everything the administrator told you about the school and its program is being implemented at the most basic level. Speak to the person on the front lines—the teacher.

Evaluating the Teacher

When you do talk with the teacher, keep your questions specific. For example, instead of asking "Do you approve of the Montessori method of teaching?" it might be better to ask "If my child came to class crying, how might you handle that?" Or "How do you deal with a child who bites others?" Find out how the teacher handles discipline, toilet training, temper tantrums, and other preschooler concerns.

A teacher's answers can help you decide how creative the staff will be in handling typical classroom issues. You can also learn a great deal about the teacher by noting how responsive the person is to your questions. If the teacher seems to be defensive or uncomfortable when answering your questions, it could signal future communication issues if there is a problem.

May I Visit During the Day?

Day visits can be more important for some children than others. Some children with a very high level of separation anxiety may benefit from visits from a parent, at least in the initial stages.

Most programs will actively encourage an open door policy that allows parents to spend more time with their children. However, the policy should be limited to reasonable times for visits such as lunch, late in the day before being picked up, and so on. Asking to visit during nap time can be potentially disturbing for other children, as they ask why *their* mom or dad didn't show up as well.

Some schools encourage parents to come and observe their children's behavior in the classroom, and for this purpose they provide either a one-way mirror or a safe corner from which to peek.

Will You Communicate with Me Daily?

It's extremely important that parent and teacher communicate daily via notes, written daily reports, chats about daily activities, and so on. The more open the lines of communication between parent and teacher, the less likely that a problem will arise unnoticed and unresolved.

You'd be surprised what a two-minute conversation can do when you stop by to pick up your child—even if rushed by a tot eager to go home—in terms of keeping you apprised of accomplishments and potential problem areas.

Daily reports can be very useful to a parent. It's nice to know how much your child ate or how long she slept. Many emotional and health problems can be prevented or taken care of with just a little bit of daily observation.

Will I Be Able to Help Make Decisions About My Child's Education?

You should be given opportunities to be involved in making decisions about the program and your child's education, and you should be encouraged to visit and observe the program at any time while your child is participating. The program also should give you community resource information and invite you to participate in educational activities. There should be a copy of the plans for the children's daily activities available for you.

May I See a Copy of the Daily Schedule?

Look for a schedule that devotes a block of time (at least 45 to 50 minutes) to exploratory play. There should also be time set aside for large and small group experiences such as story time or circle time, music, sharing news, group games, and so on.

There should be time set aside for children to play outdoors to further develop motor skills as well as social skills such as taking turns and sharing.

If your child is enrolled in an all-day preschool, check the schedule for mealtimes and snacks as well as a time planned for rest.

May I See Copies of Your Lesson Plans?

During the interview, ask to see copies of the teacher's daily, weekly, and monthly plans to get a better idea of how the teachers see the curriculum. Most of these items should be posted in visible areas, but it might help to have some copies for your own records to help you evaluate the school on your own time.

Good communication from teacher to parent—and vice versa—is absolutely crucial for ensuring your child's success at school. Better schools will be willing to share with you all their monthly, weekly, and daily lesson plans, calendars, and newsletters, together with daily notes on your child's activities.

Some schools offer parents the opportunity to help plan their child's activities with the teachers to meet the child's needs the best way possible.

Do You Schedule School Conferences?

Most preschools schedule two or three meetings during the year to discuss a child's developmental and behavioral progress. Typically, these conferences are 30 to 45 minutes long and cover a child's play style and social, language, cognitive, and physical development.

It's important to participate in these conferences because it helps you understand your growing child and shows your interest and cooperation.

If you think your work schedule will interfere with attendance, ask if you might schedule a meeting after school hours or over the telephone. A teacher-parent conference should be the time for listening and communicating openly.

Will I Be Able to Meet with or Call You?

Teachers should be available for your phone calls and meetings from time to time. In addition, parent-teacher conferences are usually scheduled several times a year, as previously discussed. These are excellent opportunities for you and the teacher to evaluate your child's progress and plan ahead for the future. Be sure to ask how many conferences the school usually schedules.

How Can I Communicate with You If I Can't Get to the School?

Many good preschools offer each family their own mailbox. This ensures privacy and is a quick and easy way to communicate important daily news in case other ways of communication aren't possible. Parents and teachers sometimes can't meet during the day because of conflicting work shifts. Some parents simply can't take off time from work to have a conference at school during business hours.

Good teachers will be sensitive to privacy issues and will be open to different views on a child's upbringing. They should be willing to try to accommodate your requests as long they are reasonable.

You should expect the teacher to get back to you quickly and discreetly with answers to questions and concerns.

Will I Be Allowed to Participate in Certain Activities?

Better programs welcome your involvement and initiative and usually offer ideas on how you can best contribute. Children, teachers, and parents all benefit tremendously when parents are part of the school.

Exactly how you might be able to participate will vary from school to school. For example, good programs are sensitive to diversity and may invite you to help teachers prepare their lessons on heritage. Or perhaps the school might ask you to read to children, volunteer on field trips, pitch in during classroom daily routines, help with a cooking lesson, fix toys, donate books and toys, or volunteer during nap or lunch time. Perhaps you could offer to host the class on a visit to your job or you might be willing to stop by and talk about what you do for a living.

Teachers never have enough time to plan and prepare for activities and especially appreciate any time you can volunteer. The administrators might appreciate your help as well, since having you stop by to proctor a class might allow them to hold a staff meeting or workshop for teachers. Don't be shy about asking how you can help the school. The better schools will likely encourage interactions, and you should seriously consider it.

Many schools provide workshops on parenting issues. Others sometimes hire parents as classroom assistants and aides, bus drivers, or office workers. These are usually part-time positions that are first offered to parents of enrolled children.

Teacher-Child Interaction

As you tour the preschool, pay close attention to the interaction between the teachers and the children, the teachers and the director, and the director and the children. Also note how the teacher and director interact with other parents, if possible.

Discipline

When children are corrected, the teacher should go to the child and speak quietly at the child's level. You don't want to see teachers shouting across the classroom unless there is an emergency.

When a problem behavior must be corrected, the teacher should discipline with logical consequences, avoiding the negative effects that follow punishment, threats, or bribes. Persistence and patience always work. Good teachers also work on preventing the undesirable behavior. The emphasis should be placed on helping children learn to take responsibility for their own behavior. If a child hits others, the teacher will talk to him or her about it calmly and suggest and model good interaction with others. If the hitting does not stop, the teacher should be persistent until it does.

It is quite possible that there will be a child with some emotional problem, a child who is unusually strong willed, or a child with special needs. Or perhaps there will be a child who simply enjoys the benefits of being a "trouble maker" and likes to test both teachers and classmates. All these examples are usual challenges every teacher encounters at some point. However, if the teacher is firm about the rules and has good self-control, most simple discipline guidelines will be effective. Children generally respond well to this way of correcting negative behavior.

Ask your teacher to alert you to any unusual behavior your child exhibits. This can be a sign of many things; children "act up" when sick, tired, or have fears and concerns. Chances are that good teachers, who know this, will contact you right away. If the problem behavior is treated in the same positive way at home and at school, your child will be "cured" much faster. Good preschools don't use any type of physical or corporal punishment, and they don't link punishment to food, bathroom use, or naps. Preschools should have a policy of zero tolerance for teachers who engage in corporal punishment. Harsh, shaming, or insulting behavior should not be tolerated.

Ideally, emphasis should be placed on preventing incidents in the first place by keeping children busy with challenging and interesting activities and by helping children develop their own problem-solving skills.

These days, the "time-out" disciplinary technique so popular several years ago is considered ineffective. You'll find it used much less frequently these days.

Respect
You should see adults using a respectful tone of voice when talking with children at the preschool, and the children should also show respect in communicating with adults and other children.

Teachers earn respect by immediately responding to the children's needs and by showing a sincere interest in children as they listen, make eye contact, play, laugh, smile, hug, and hold a child.

An Atmosphere of Warmth
As you visit the preschool, you should notice a sense of mutual caring and liking throughout the center. You should see a sense of unconditional

acceptance and positive regard. Adults should listen to, talk with, and frequently touch children in a caring way.

Encouragement

As you spend time at the school, you should notice encouragement and affirmation being freely offered. You want to look for a "you can do it" or "I have confidence in you" attitude from the teachers toward the students.

Independence

Although teachers should be supportive and warm, you should not see them trying to improve on or finish a child's projects. Children should not be expected to perform beyond their level of capability, but the teacher shouldn't do things for the children that they are perfectly capable of doing themselves.

Positive Focus

Teachers should direct students with positive statements that focus on what *needs* to be done as opposed to what *shouldn't* be done. You should hear "The Legos need to be put in this box," not "Don't leave the Legos on the table."

Recognition of Progress

Teachers should be recognizing and encouraging children for the progress they've made on a project. You should see art being pinned up on the board, teachers making appreciative comments on a child's process, and so on.

Acceptance of Mistakes

Mistakes are a way of learning. Children who aren't making any mistakes aren't likely taking chances in volunteering information. If a child spills milk because of inattention while you're observing the class, the teacher should not criticize the child for making a mistake. Instead, the teacher should simply ask what the child could do differently next time to avoid that mistake and ask the child to help clean up the spilled milk.

Encouraging Responsibility

Teachers should give each child an opportunity to build responsibility and contribute to the group by passing out paper or snacks, feeding a class pet, washing the board, or wiping the table after a meal.

Empowering Through Choices

You should see plenty of opportunity for preschoolers to make simple choices whenever possible and practical. Making choices empowers young children by giving them some control over their life.

Fostering Negotiation Skills

When children disagree over whose turn it is or which toy to play with, the teacher should hand over the responsibility for settling the problem to the children. The teacher might say something like "When you two can decide how you can get along and play with this together, let me know and I'll be happy to give it to you. Until then, it must be put away."

Pick-Up Time

Try to visit during the end of the day, so you can observe what happens when parents pick up their children. Teachers and administrators should be supportive by sharing with parents at least one positive thing that occurred during the day. Reports about incidents of unacceptable behavior should never be discussed when any child is present.

In the Next Chapter

Now you've got a good idea of the kind of questions you should be asking the teachers and directors. In the next chapter, you'll learn what to expect when it comes to assessing your child.

Chapter 8

Assessing and Testing
Your Preschooler

Children's abilities and performances differ a great deal, and these differences are obvious in social environments like preschools. Even though evaluating children's progress in all areas is important, standardized tests don't often reveal the true knowledge and abilities of young children. It is also unfair, to say the least, to use such unreliable and outdated tests for detecting special needs.

The importance of assessing children is often misunderstood. Although we try to determine the validity of tests and create some kind of accountability system, the true purpose—to improve the quality of teaching and learning—is overlooked in favor of statistics that can be quite inaccurate.

The outcomes of testing depend on many factors that cannot be ignored. Neglecting such factors could produce misleading results. For instance, tests created more than 20 years ago cannot be considered reliable simply because demographics and technology have changed. Old standardized tests may not be flexible enough to accurately portray the language or social skills of many children coming from different cultures. Nor can this kind of testing evaluate children whose computer skills may exceed the average.

As a parent, you must have asked yourself more than once whether your child's development and learning are on track. Your anxiousness is understandable—you need correct answers. After all, you should know what your children's potentials are so you can steer them in the right direction.

Assessments

One way of improving the overall quality of early childhood education and the potential for every child's development is for teachers to conduct carefully planned assessments.

An assessment is an ongoing evaluation of a child's progress by observing the child and communicating with families. Daily observation is an important way to keep track of each child's development.

The purpose of assessments in a preschool setting is not to find out who is "smart" and who is "dumb," but to help teachers create a positive learning environment for each child. Even though some common developmental milestones are reached at the preschool age, every child is an individual and develops at his or her own pace. Assessments help teachers find out what areas children excel in and what areas they might need to focus on.

Teachers observe appropriate classroom activities and document the work children do and the way they do it. All assessments done in the classroom should be sensitive to each child's needs, learning abilities, language the child speaks at home, and current developmental stage. Children should be observed in different settings and situations, so only typical behavior is considered as a valid indicator of each child's progress.

Assessing a child's development in a preschool should be systematic and should include all areas of early childhood development—social, emotional, creative, physical, and so on.

These observations are also used to identify children with special needs. Commonly used classroom interventions can be successful at providing proper care for a child with special needs. Occasionally, however, teachers consider a referral for an evaluation by the district's special needs services.

Any information is valuable, and when observing, a teacher will study each child's behavior in the group (whether the children withdraw, how they communicate with peers, how they place themselves in the classroom), how they solve conflicts or other problems, individual interests, and so on.

Carefully formulated checklists, behavioral descriptions, and techniques such as writing down anecdotes, conversations, or comments are all good tools for assessing a child's development. Checklists, forms, or questionnaires should document each child's progress toward the developmental goal.

Teachers integrate the results of assessments into curriculum planning and use the information to adapt teaching practices and help children who might need additional time or assistance in certain areas.

Finally, teachers gather a child's work and experiences at school to share with the child's family, along with their assessment of the child's progress. Videotapes and photos are handy additions to the individual portfolios teachers should create for all children. These collections should also include samples of drawings and other artwork as well as dictated stories and/or audiotapes with the child's comments. It's important that all the collected material gives a clear idea about the child's overall development.

When presenting the portfolios to a child's family or communicating news on a daily basis, you should expect teachers to stress the positive. While explaining the importance of assessments in every area of a child's development, your child's teachers will support their observations and comments with collected material.

You should expect the teacher to listen carefully to your input because parent-teacher cooperation is essential in identifying the needs your child might have.

When working with children, teachers should respect children's self-assessments and their input. Children respond in different ways to assessment; while some might feel comfortable with standard interviews, others will respond better during an activity.

Whatever the case, the teacher's assessments should consist of accurate statements reflecting your child's overall development and be used only for the purpose of creating a better learning environment for each child.

Standardized Testing

There has been a lot of talk about standardized testing of young children aged three to eight. Although many educators agree that using standardized tests for young children can be inaccurate and very harmful to them, these tests are still being used.

Testing is sometimes conducted merely to document a young child's achievements. The results of such testing are often used to limit entry into especially competitive school programs. Rejection at an early age cannot be a good start for anyone, yet in some states many parents insist on such use of standardized testing and even hire tutors or buy prepared questions and answers so their youngsters can "score" well.

Young children don't usually respond well to standardized tests. They don't understand the significance of testing and, therefore, don't always perform to their full potential. Their attention spans are short, and many have problems following multi-step directions. In most cases, children feel pressured, don't finish given projects, and sometimes get bored.

Generally, testing of young children consists of several parts, including a verbal test to determine language development and general knowledge about the world and a performance test to examine how children use their hands to manipulate objects and solve problems.

Verbal Tests

During the verbal part of the test, children are asked general questions, showing their ability to express themselves and present general knowledge about their environment. For instance, the tester might evaluate the child's comprehension level by asking simple questions such as "Why do we need cars?" or "Why do plants need water?"

Understanding what words mean is always a more difficult task than just being able to repeat a word. Verbal comprehension will definitely impress the tester evaluating the vocabulary.

Mathematics

While being tested in arithmetic, children will be asked to count objects and probably solve a few math problems out loud.

A child's ability to comprehend similarities and differences is another item on the testing menu. Standard questions include "What is bigger, smaller, the same, or different?"

Performance Tests

Performance tests are usually more fun for children to do, but not every child is always in the mood for mazes, blocks, or puzzles. Needless to say, this greatly affects the results of the testing. Also, some children sense the importance of the testing and feel even more stressed and intimidated.

Children are expected to copy block designs, assemble puzzles, complete pictures, copy printed geometric designs, and solve mazes. While children are performing, the tester examines their hand-eye coordination, fine motor skills, and ability to think and react.

In the long run, there is always the chance that the results of such testing throughout the preschool years can damage a child's self-image and inhibit learning abilities, aside from the fact that it doesn't always accurately reflect the level of knowledge or quality of education they receive.

If a preschool you're considering requires this type of standardized testing, ask yourself if you really want to subject your child to the possibility of failure. Is it possible to assess a three- or four-year-old in a couple hours? Do you really want your child to attend a school that relies on standardized tests? If that's their attitude toward learning, what makes them so prestigious? How often does the testing lead to mislabeling children?

Even though many studies reveal that children can experience a high level of stress during standardized group testing, many test designers claim that this kind of assessment is more objective than documentation supported by intentional daily observation. However, many states are seriously rethinking their policies on testing and school-readiness assessments.

Experts do agree that the quality of an age-appropriate curriculum and the quality of care and individual attention offered in classrooms are crucial for every child's achievement. Consistent individual observation and documentation provide the best chance for bringing about positive and accurate results and helping children achieve.

In the Next Chapter

In the next chapter, parents of children with special needs can learn what to expect as they consider preschools.

Chapter 9

If Your Child Has Special Needs

We all know that children develop at different rates. Many parents begin comparing their child to other children almost immediately. By the age of two or three, children who aren't developing quite on track compared to most of their peers should be showing signs of trouble.

Parents who notice any of the following signs in their child should consult a pediatrician or other specialist as soon as possible, as they could indicate potential special needs problems:

- Tires quickly
- Has trouble eating or sleeping
- Is unable to focus on a task for more than a few seconds
- Is awkward or clumsy
- Has difficulty running, jumping, hopping, climbing, throwing or catching a ball, or riding a tricycle
- Is fearful of new situations or people
- Is extremely shy

- Avoids interactions with others
- Is socially withdrawn
- Is not interested in playing with other children
- Has trouble using crayons, large pencils, or scissors
- Has trouble picking up small objects
- Doesn't communicate well
- Doesn't understand what things go together (such as shirts and pants or socks and shoes)
- Is moody
- Is aggressive
- Has poor self-control

There's a lot of confusion and controversy around special education, especially in the area of preschool education. Unfortunately, children with special needs and their families are the ones most often caught in the middle.

It is also unfortunate that many don't understand or can't foresee the importance of good quality preschool education for children with disabilities.

Americans with Disabilities Act

If you're a parent with a special needs child, you may already be familiar with the Americans with Disabilities Act (ADA), which gives civil rights protections to people with disabilities. Title III of this document states that almost all public spaces such as hotels, restaurants, banks, schools, movie theaters, and so on, must provide reasonable accommodations for people with disabilities. With the exception of preschool centers that are sponsored by religious organizations such as churches, synagogues, and mosques, almost every other child-care setting must comply with this law.

According to Title III of the ADA, there are regulations with which every preschool must comply. Here are some specific requirements:

- Preschools can't discriminate against children with special needs and exclude them from their programs, unless the disabilities pose a direct threat to the health and safety of others and/or require fundamental alteration of the program.

- Preschools must make "reasonable adjustments and modifications" to their programs to be able to include children, parents, and guardians with disabilities.

- Preschools must make their facilities physically accessible to people with disabilities and provide sufficient aid in accommodating children with various types of disabilities without charging "excessive costs."

Preschool providers are in most cases ready to accommodate their programs and facilities, but they aren't always knowledgeable about the process of adapting their schools and curriculum appropriately.

According to the ADA Title III, preschools should evaluate their programs and determine how and what needs to be done to successfully include children with disabilities. They must not simply assume that a child's disability is "too severe."

Instead, an individual assessment must be completed and should never be based on stereotypes and preconceptions about what children with disabilities can or cannot do. During this assessment, the teacher should always include parents, other educators, and health-care professionals who have come in contact with the child. A team of educators creates an Individual Educational Plan (IEP) to determine whether the regular classroom is an appropriate and beneficial environment for the child with disability. The purpose of this approach is to educate as many disabled children as possible in regular education environments.

The Reauthorization of the Individuals with Disabilities Education Act (IDEA) places greater emphasis on the participation of children with disabilities in the general education curriculum. The 1997 Amendments to IDEA require that the IEP include a statement of the child's present level of educational performance, including how the disability affects the child's participation in appropriate activities.

After the IEP has been created, reasonable effort should be made to include the child in the regular program. A denial will be considered only if it is determined that the child will not benefit from enrolling and the disability is in any way threatening to others. Denial on this basis is the most common reason for excluding a special needs child from a regular education program.

The second most common reason for excluding a child with special needs from a regular educational program is usually related to the cost of care or adapting the facilities. Insurance companies that cover preschools often raise their rates if disabled children are going to be admitted. According to Title III, cost is not a valid reason for denial. The law suggests that every extra cost be evenly distributed among all tuition-paying families.

In addition, preschools may be eligible for tax credits or deductions offered to businesses (particularly small businesses) by the Internal Revenue Service in compliance with Americans with Disabilities Act regulations.

Preschool teachers often worry that children with disabilities require more individual attention and that this might be a problem because the staff will not have enough time for other children. This can be considered a valid reason only if the disability is seriously time-consuming, fundamentally alters the program, or creates an unrealistic cost of care.

Other concerns, such as the need for toileting assistance, are usually easily solved. Many schools will provide and even adapt existing space for toileting needs. For example, even if the preschool generally doesn't accept children if not toilet trained, under most state regulations these services must be provided for a child with special needs, and strict hygiene requirements should be followed.

Delayed speech and other developmental delays are not legitimate reasons for exclusion from a preschool program. These special needs children should always be placed in age-appropriate classrooms, because research suggests that in most cases, children with developmental delays benefit from contact with peers in regular educational environments.

Some schools have strict policies about administering medication, and children with severe and life-threatening allergies might pose a challenge in preschools. However, the ADA states that as long as reasonable precaution and care are used while administering medications, caregivers are generally not liable for any resulting complications.

Mobility, vision, and hearing problems are on the list of disabilities that can be easily included in regular educational settings. If reasonable adjustments have been made, there should not be a problem with allowing these children to attend preschool. For instance, even if a school has a no-pets policy, a visually impaired child is allowed to bring a guide dog. Children wearing leg or arm braces should be helped properly, as long as other children are not left unattended.

Parents or guardians with disabilities should also be accommodated by providing reasonable ways of communication (such as an interpreter), as long as it is not excessively expensive and at the cost of the child's family.

Inclusion

Educators don't all agree on the benefits of having a child with special needs included in a regular classroom. Some experts believe that children with disabilities should first start in a special education classroom and gradually "earn" their way to regular education. They also believe that partial participation in regular education environments, where students with disabilities are allowed to share space with peers but not necessarily participate in activities, is enough to satisfy the law.

Other experts insist that children with disabilities belong and should begin education in regular classrooms as long as the appropriate services can be provided and the children are benefiting from the program.

There are two federal laws specifically designed to govern education of children with disabilities. Neither of them *requires* inclusion, but both laws insist on providing the proper inclusive *environment*.

The Office of Special Education Programs (OSEP) has, since 1997, been administering the Individuals with Disabilities Act (IDEA). IDEA requires that children with disabilities be educated "to the maximum extent appropriate in the least restrictive environment." In the case of preschools, the "least restrictive environment" would be a regular education classroom.

Section 504 of the Rehabilitation Act was created in 1973 and has since financially supported educational organizations and institutions. Under this law, all affected preschools are obligated to provide reasonable accommodations for children with disabilities at no extra cost to families. These requirements apply to subsidized child-care centers, recreational programs, before- and after-school programs, and summer programs.

Several studies conducted in the late 1980s show that the employment rate of high school students with disabilities educated in inclusive programs was significantly higher than the employment rate of students from segregated special education programs. Further, the same research shows that the cost of educating children in special schools was double that of educating them in inclusive programs.

Finding the Right Solution

The first step in finding the right solution for your child with special needs should begin with gathering information from your local school board and their special services department. They are obligated under law to assist parents of special needs children.

They will also conduct all necessary consultations and evaluations by providing qualified staff. If it's determined that your child will benefit from attending a regular preschool, make a list of all preschools you know of or the ones recommended to you and contact them. For additional listings, call your local district's resource and referral agencies.

If your child is accepted into the program, you might be asked to provide some cooperation and, if necessary, an aid who will accompany your child during the school hours. If this is not an affordable option for you, inquire about other possibilities with the special services department. This is where you will find information about many issues such as transportation and financial help.

States and local district organizations may have different rules and regulations about children with special needs, and the financial help varies. Don't stop asking questions, however. This area is presently undergoing changes in policies and regulations, and these greatly depend on individual cases.

Before visiting preschools, refer to all characteristics of a good program discussed in this book and then ask the school administrator what kinds of necessary changes or adaptations the school will want to make. Be sure to specify your child's special needs. If for instance, your child uses a wheelchair, ask how the toileting might be arranged and, of course, look for wheelchair access.

The curriculum for young children with disabilities should provide experiences in a wide range of activities as well as provide opportunities to interact with the environment in a meaningful context.

A critical issue is whether the curriculum teaches the special needs child the functional skills the child needs to learn. The program philosophy and beliefs about how young children learn will also greatly influence the curriculum. Your best bet is to maintain close communication with the school. This will help both you and the school in determining whether your child is benefiting from the program.

Don't dismiss your child's signs of readiness for preschool. Children with special needs who haven't had any contacts with large groups of peers or have spent most part of their early years nurtured at home might be in particular intimidated by preschools. If this is the case, look for smaller schools with fewer children and more intense staff supervision. Also be sensitive to the fact that your older preschooler might feel "different." Most regular preschools do a great job of accepting and absorbing children with special needs into their programs. Their positive attitudes will reflect on their teaching. Work closely with teachers, and keep encouraging your child every step of the way.

The type of curriculum used in an early childhood program must respond to the strengths and needs of individual children. When working with young children with disabilities, teachers must emphasize communication and social skills development—areas that can be taught within the broad context of appropriate learning environments for all children.

In the Next Chapter

In the next chapter, you'll learn how to prepare your child for preschool, how to introduce the idea, and how to handle the first anxiety-provoking days.

Chapter 10

Is Your Child Ready for Preschool?

Charline was interested in starting her two-year-old son Justin at her local preschool, but she wasn't sure whether he was really ready. He was a bright child, but he was reluctant to separate from her and wasn't used to playing in groups of children.

As Charline discovered, most preschools will start accepting children at about age two—but just because your child will be old enough by September doesn't mean it's automatically time for preschool. Not all children of two or even three are ready for preschool, even if every other child on your block seems more than prepared.

Encountering a new preschool environment with unfamiliar teachers and strange children can make your child feel anxious and excited at the same time. You may be having mixed emotions about whether your child is ready for preschool.

The more comfortable you are as a parent about your decision to place your child in preschool and the more familiar the setting can be made for your child, the fewer problems you—and your child—will face.

Preschool Readiness

"Preschool readiness" has to do with whether a child is socially, emotionally, physically, and cognitively ready to participate in a daily, structured, educational program with a group of other children. It's tempting to read a list of skills and say "Yes, my child can do these things, he's ready!" Perhaps he is—but perhaps he isn't.

Preschoolers need some social activities, and most will enjoy playing with others as they begin to learn how to make friends. But preschool may not be appropriate for all children; some need an extra year of unstructured play at home before venturing out into school.

Children benefit from being in a stimulating environment at an early age, but not all children are ready for preschool at age two or three. You're really the best judge of when to send your child.

What Are Your Motives?

The best way to decide if preschool is right for your child is to ask yourself honestly why you want him to start preschool now. Do you think your child needs to play with others, or are you looking for a way to get him out of your hair for a few hours? Are you worried that every other child on the block is going, and you don't want your daughter to be left out? Is your mother or your best friend pressuring you to enroll your child?

Are you hoping to get your child into the "right" preschool now so he'll be eligible for the "right" gifted program later on? Think about your child's personality and talk to other people who know him well, such as your spouse and your child's pediatrician. Make sure you consider preschool for the best reasons for your child.

Are you worried that if you don't enroll him in preschool he won't be ready for kindergarten? Most experts agree that there are plenty of other ways for children to develop the skills necessary to be successful in kindergarten, including attending a good daycare facility or spending quality time at home with you or another loving caregiver.

A study by the National Institutes of Child Health and Human Development found that children do best if they're cared for by someone who is genuinely concerned about their well-being and development and who makes sure they're doing a variety of age-appropriate activities. They don't need to be enrolled in preschool for that.

Your Child Is Ready If …

It's probably the perfect time to choose a preschool if you find that your child seems eager to learn new things and explore or isn't getting enough stimulation at home or in daycare. Perhaps your child seems ready to interact with other children and eager to make new friends. If this is the case, chances are it's the perfect time to start school.

One way to judge whether your child is ready is to assess a range of skills and traits that are crucial for a good adjustment in a preschool:

- Is your child developing a sense of independence—can she wash her hands, eat independently, and sleep and go to the bathroom alone?
- Can your child easily separate from you?
- Can your child work on projects alone?
- Does your child enjoy group activities?
- Can your child follow a routine?
- Does your child have the stamina for preschool?
- Does your child's personality suggest that is he emotionally ready?
- Is your child ready to learn? Is his or her cognitive development on track?

Let's examine each of these points more closely and ask what you can do to prepare your child for the big jump to preschool.

Independence

Preschool requires children to have certain basic skills, and independence is one of the most important. First of all, most schools will expect your child to be toilet trained. If your child is still wearing a diaper most of the time, most preschools would require you to wait. In addition, your child should be able to take care of other basic personal needs, such as washing hands after painting, eating lunch without help, and sleeping alone.

What You Can Do

Provide a lot of self-help experiences for your child. If she would rather have you feed her than feed herself, the best approach is to give her fun-shape, child-size utensils, dishes, or drinking cups. Children readily give up their dependence for colorful juice boxes with silly straws.

If your three-year-old is still attached to his bottle or a pacifier, begin limiting the use gradually.

If you are toilet training your child, make sure that he or she is not rushed. Be consistent and see that this important project does not coincide with the first days of preschool. If your child feels pressured, be ready for setbacks.

Separation

Has your child been in daycare before or been cared for by a relative? If not, think about how easily your child separates from you. Is there a problem if you leave the child with a baby-sitter or even a family member?

When you consider preschool, your child's readiness to separate from you is very important. Is your child able to separate without copious tears? Has he spent time away from you? Can she work on projects on her own? Is your child ready to participate in group activities and follow a regular schedule?

If your child has been cared for by a baby-sitter or a relative all along, he'll probably be better prepared to separate from you when it's time for preschool. Children who are used to being apart from their parents often move right into preschool with no hesitation at all. On the other hand, children who have spent all their time up to this point with one of their parents during the day may have a harder time suddenly leaving that intense one-on-one relationship.

If your child hasn't had many opportunities to be away from you up to this point, you might want to think about scheduling some time apart.

Many children leave their primary caregiving parent for the first time when it's time for preschool, and they handle the separation just fine. The trick is to help your child adjust to separation for brief periods. Many pre-schools will allow you to drop your child off for an hour or so during the first few days of school. Then, as your child gets used to the school environment, you can slowly increase the time he spends there.

Some experts believe that preschool may be particularly important for children who haven't had any caregivers other than a parent, in preparation for the move to kindergarten.

What You Can Do

Start encouraging the signs of independence such as playing alone for longer periods of time or going for a short walk with Grandpa. Gradually extend the time you are separated; your child will have more time to enjoy the company of and develop routines with your "substitute." Think about leaving your child for a day with your sister or other close relative and their children.

Introduce him to other children and have play-dates, and never forget to prepare your child enthusiastically about what will follow. Whenever you can, engage your child in making short-term plans. By casually saying "Tomorrow is a school day. Would you help me make your lunch in the morning?" you will shift the focus from separation to what is more fun to do.

Chances are that your child will quickly learn to have fun with others. Do not become overly "soft" to your child's tears. It is okay for children to feel sad when separating from you. The message you should be sending to your child is simple: "Don't worry, have fun, I love you, and see you later."

Works Alone

Is your child able to work on projects independently? Preschool programs usually focus on lots of arts and crafts projects that require concentration and the ability to focus on an individual task. If your child really loves to draw and paint at home, enjoys creative arts and crafts projects, or gets engrossed in puzzles and other activities independently, odds are he's ready for preschool.

What You Can Do

Even if your child is the type who asks for help with everything, you can start getting him ready by setting up playtimes where he can entertain himself for a half hour or so. While you wash the dishes, encourage him to make creatures out of clay, for example.

Gradually build up to longer stretches of solo play. Your goal here is to keep yourself moderately preoccupied with an activity so he'll get on with his own without too much hand-holding from you.

Participates in a Group

Is he ready to participate in group activities? Many preschool activities, such as "circle time," require that all the children in a class participate at the same time. These interactions give children a chance to play and learn together, but also require them to sit still, listen to stories, and sing songs.

This can be very difficult for kids under three, who are naturally active explorers and not always developmentally ready to play with other children.

All preschool children have to get along with other kids. If your child isn't used to group activities, then activities such as sharing, taking turns, and playing cooperatively can be very difficult.

What You Can Do

You can start introducing your child to group activities yourself. Help your child get used to being part of a group by arranging play dates with one or two peers or enrolling him in a music class to help him get used to playing with other children. Take him to story time at your local library, for instance, or sign him up for a class such as tumbling.

Follows Routines

Preschools usually follow a predictable routine: circle time, play time, snack, playground, then lunch. There's a good reason for this. Children tend to feel most comfortable and in control when the same things happen at the same time each day.

What You Can Do

If your child doesn't keep to a schedule and each day is different from the last, it can help to standardize his days a bit before he starts preschool. Start by offering meals on a regular timetable. You could also plan to visit the park each afternoon. Add a "story time" right after lunch, for example, or "quiet time" after playing in the yard.

If you take it a step farther and adopt his program's basic schedule for a couple weeks before his first day, you'll help him slip easily into the routine.

You also should set—and stick to—a bedtime ritual (bath, then books, then bed).

Has Stamina

Whether it's a half-day or full-day program, preschool can be a tiring place. There are art projects to do, field trips to take, and playgrounds to explore. Does your child thrive on activities like this, or does he have trouble moving from one thing to the next without getting cranky?

You also need to think about naps and when your child needs to sleep. Preschools usually schedule a nap time after lunch. If your child has no problem with nap times in the afternoon—or has already abandoned nap time—she'll be fine. But if your child still crashes mid-morning, it might be too soon to think about enrolling her in preschool.

What You Can Do

You can work toward building up your child's stamina by making sure she gets a good night's sleep. If you have some flexibility in your schedule, you might also want to start your child off with a half-day program to ease into the excitement of preschool life, gradually increasing the length of the school day as your child gets more comfortable.

Is Ready for Learning

There are probably lots of things on your mind concerning your child's learning. Perhaps you are worried that learning two different languages spoken at home might somehow interfere with your child's understanding of any of them. Perhaps you would want your child to be good with math, but his favorite activity is painting.

You have seen that some children love puzzles, but yours couldn't care less. Does your child like to hold books and look at them? Does your three-year-old engage in pretend play or like to sing songs? Has he or she begun to recognize colors and shapes?

The next factor to consider is your child's personality. Is your child active and outspoken or quiet and shy? Does she get upset easily, or does nothing ever seem to bother her? Will your only child ever learn how to share?

You know these questions must be answered before starting preschool. Whether you choose a structured or unstructured program will depend on your child.

Well, you're ready to prepare your child for a good start. But how?

What You Can Do

If it's true that learning never stops, then childhood is just a fast-forward version of this process. Your only concern should be what, when, and how much you should offer to your child. If everything is on track developmentally, especially cognition, you can continue introducing meaningful things to your child. Remember that children learn through play and that fun must be the biggest part of any activity. This is the best way to introduce new things and preserve your child's endless curiosity.

So read and talk to them and play with them a lot. Take them places and let them meet other children. Encourage them to try new things.

Easing the Transition

Adjusting to preschool can be tough for any child, even one who's been in daycare for a while. You can help ease your child's transition to preschool with the following ideas and activities.

Learn as much as possible about the school before your child's first day, so you can answer her questions about it. And make a point of telling her in a matter-of-fact tone about some of the fun activities she'll get to take part in, either in the classroom or on the playground. If the school takes special field trips or has class animals, this may help interest your child.

Before the first day of preschool, gradually introduce your child to activities commonly offered in a preschool classroom. A child accustomed to scribbling with paper and crayons at home, for example, will find it comforting to discover the same crayons and paper in the preschool classroom.

The important thing is to keep any preparation fun. At this age, learning shouldn't be a chore. You don't want your child to feel like every activity is a lesson or every outing an educational field trip.

Set Up Some Play Dates

It's a good idea to give your child lots of experience in playing with other children the same age before starting a formal preschool program. The more comfortable your child feels around other children, the easier the adjustment will be. This won't be hard if you live in the city or suburbs with lots of children around, but rural parents may have to work a bit harder to set up play dates.

Initial play dates for children aged $2^{1}/_{2}$ to $3^{1}/_{2}$ should be fairly short—just about 45 minutes to an hour. You can increase this up to about $1^{1}/_{2}$ hours for 4- and 5-year-olds who are just getting to know each other.

It's much better to have the play date end when the children are still having fun and don't want to leave, rather than to have the play date stretch on too long until fatigue sets in and triggers disagreements.

Be sure to include snacks and plenty of supervision for two- and three-year-olds—they just may not play quite so well with each other as do children aged four or five. It's still important for them to have experiences playing in the same room with same-age children and sharing toys, however.

If you're going to invite another toddler (two- to three-year-old) to your home, make sure you get prepared first. Put away any really special toys you know your child won't want to share, and include plenty of similar toys so there won't be any arguments.

Read to Your Child

Most preschool classes schedule at least one reading period each day. Setting aside at least 15 minutes daily at home for reading will make this seem like a familiar ritual to your child when preschool begins.

There are lots of stories you can find that feature young children or animal characters who anticipate their first day of preschool. Look for the books describing the anticipation, the worries, and the excitement of that very first day. They should have happy endings, with children meeting nice teachers, making new friends, and having fun.

Remember, children who don't have early experiences with books often have more problems in learning to read later on. Experts always stress that reading to your child is the best way to ensure your child will be successful in school.

Preschool children enjoy books with colorful illustrations, repetitive language patterns, "please touch" pages, pop-ups, and interactive materials.

Young children may not have the attention span to follow a very detailed story, but most children enjoy the melody of rhymes. This is why Dr. Seuss books are such favorites; these simple-to-understand books use silly rhymes and phrases to teach colors, shapes, and numbers. You can use books like these to snag a young child's interest in reading and in learning.

Because preschoolers can't read on their own, they need to learn to listen. Reading aloud to your child is also a great way to help her develop good listening skills.

Stories with rhythm are particularly engaging, so look for books that repeat phrases. When he starts remembering the phrases, ask him to "read" with you and let him fill in the repetitive parts he knows by heart.

Your child will also learn to predict the outcome of a story in preschool. To help prepare for this, you can stop midway through a book and ask questions about what your child thinks will happen next or how the story might end.

Listening Skills

Preschool teachers often encourage their busy young students to sit still, close their eyes, and listen. You can help your child prepare for this request by sometimes suggesting she sit quietly and close her eyes and tell you all the different sounds she hears. This is particularly easy if you're outdoors in nature during the summer. Talk about what's making the sounds and where the sounds are coming from.

Sequencing

In preschool, children learn to listen and follow multi-step directions. You can help prepare your child for this by asking him to perform a series of requests, such as taking a coat to the hall and putting it in the closet, or going into the kitchen to get the silverware and then coming to the dining room to help you set the table.

Your child will enjoy games that involve listening to directions and solving problems. While waiting for the doctor to come, you can play the I Spy game—giving hints about an object in the office that you see. "I spy with my little eye something that is ... silver." Your child then asks you questions about the object until he correctly guesses what the object is. Simon Says is another good listening game that all preschoolers really love to play. Try this one with several neighborhood children to multiply the fun.

Board games are another good way to reinforce sequencing. You can use board games, computer games—or invent your own (*first* you roll the dice, *then* you move, *then* you follow the directions on the space ...).

Playing board games also teaches sportsmanship and patience because children must wait their turn to roll the dice or move a game piece.

Working with Art

Art—whether it's finger-painting, making potholders, or drawing pictures—helps preschoolers develop the visual and fine motor skills they will need when it's time to learn to write.

Keep plenty of paper, markers, paint, crayons, crafts, and other art supplies on hand and encourage your child to create. Encourage your child's creativity by using Silly Putty, Play-Doh, and clay. This teaches a child to be creative while improving dexterity as they hold and use pencils and crayons. Silly Putty, Play-Doh, and clay also enhance coordination by requiring a child to use hands, eyes, and the mind to create an object.

Many children love simple mazes, and working on mazes or connect-the-dot pictures will also help your child develop beginning writing skills.

Following Directions

Give your child some practice in following simple directions, cooperating with others, and making choices. If you can, make a game out of the learning process—or at least don't get scolding and fierce. Remember that most children will behave better for their teachers than for their parents, so don't worry if your child resists.

Don't expect your child to do all the work; you can keep it easygoing by helping out. The two of you can take turns putting pieces into a puzzle or putting things away in his room. Or try giving your child some fun instructions ("pick out a marker and draw a cat") or play Simon Says.

When you present choices, be specific and limit the number of options: "Do you want to color a picture or play with your dolls?"

Real-Life Experiences

Another good way to promote preschool readiness is by having your child participate in some real-life experiences, such as helping to set the table or fold the laundry. These chores will help teach responsibility—and experts also have found that hands-on learning and real-life experiences are vital for early learning. Children learn by *doing* and *exploring*.

Expose your child to lots of real-life experiences. Take him along on family trips to the museum, zoo, park, farm, store, fair, circus, and library.

Freedom to Experiment

Giving a child plenty of freedom to experiment is important. Research suggests that experimenting with options helps a child develop a foundation for school readiness as well as lifelong achievement. Have him drop a ball and a feather. Which falls faster? Have her fill up a bowl using funnels of different sizes. What happens? Have her pour water into a bowl of baking soda. What does she think might occur?

Set Up a Routine

Especially if you've been operating a fairly laissez-faire atmosphere in your home, it may be a good idea in the summer before preschool to establish a basic routine for your child at home.

You certainly don't have to come up with a rigid schedule of activities exactly like a typical preschool day (free play, clean up, snack, circle time, art, recess, lunch, and nap time). Instead, aim for a simple set of rules and expectations that will help your child adjust to the preschool experience.

Insist that your child begin to put away toys or craft materials after he's finished playing with them. Have a quiet story time after lunch. Require that materials be treated with respect. If your child doesn't treat a game or toy properly or safely, put it away for a specified period of time.

Talk

It may sound odd to tell parents to simply talk to their children, but many families get so caught up in everyday life that precious little real communication takes place.

Talking to children helps them acquire and extend their use of language. Talk with them as you read together, take walks, eat and play together, or drive to the store together.

You may not realize how much learning can go on just by your talking out loud. For example, if your child is helping you bake brownies, try thinking out loud: "We need two cups of flour. But all I have is this half-cup measure. I know that two of these equals one cup. So I guess I'll need four half cups. Do you see that two of these make one whole cup?"

Or while you're shopping, talk out loud to your child as you go: "I'd like to buy oranges for our lunch. There is just the two of us. But these oranges are selling for three for a dollar. If you ate one orange and I ate one orange, how could we split this last orange?"

Children this age also love to ask questions: Why? How? You can use their curiosity as a teaching tool. To get them interested in something, ask a question. It doesn't have to have an easy answer—something like "I wonder why the ocean looks blue?"

Talk to your child about daily activities. It enhances your relationship and helps your child summarize the experiences. Asking questions like "What did you do today?" will most likely provoke a "Nothing" answer—so instead, prompt them with open-ended questions such as "Did you play tag at Suzy's house today? Did you see your friend Johnny? What did you have for snack?"

And remember—it's not enough to ask the questions—you've got to listen to the answers, too.

Scientists have discovered critical links between speaking, reading, and writing. How you use language will directly influence how your child uses language. Use words to label everything. Use rhythm, rhyme, and adult vocabulary. Young children love big words!

Music

Because children also enjoy songs and music, these make great teaching tools. Popular TV programs like *Barney* and *Sesame Street* use music and songs to entertain while teaching—you can, too. Singing is also a good way to help build a child's memory skills.

Set Boundaries

There's not a thing wrong with the word "no." Don't be afraid to use that word when it's appropriate, because setting boundaries for appropriate behavior and activities helps children feel safe and secure.

Broaching the Subject

When you've finally reached a decision about whether your child is ready for preschool (and have decided on which preschool is best for your child), you'll want to discuss the upcoming new experience and how excited you are about it. If you feel safe and secure about a preschool and can pass that feeling on to your child, when September comes your child will feel safe and secure, too.

But don't raise your child's anxiety by starting to talk about preschool too far in advance. Even though it's good to announce things to children, they deal better with the unknown on much shorter notice.

Introduce the idea gradually, especially if your child has never attended preschool before. Mention it here and there and ask questions like "What do you think you would like to play with in school?"

Most schools don't mind if children bring a favorite object, like a small toy or book, that can serve as a bit of home during the adjustment period. It's a good idea to wait for a child to ask for such a transition object rather than to suggest it yourself, however.

It's not a good idea for adults to behave as though they agree with the child that a tattered old threadbare blanket can keep her safe, but there's nothing wrong with respecting a child's desire to cling to something familiar in times of stress. Most children spontaneously give up these symbolic comforts by the time they enter kindergarten.

Your child may want to know why you want him to go to preschool. Explain that you think it will be a good opportunity to play with a variety of toys you don't have at home and that it will be a chance to make new friends and be a "big kid." Make sure to tell your child how proud you are because he or she is a big boy or girl now. Let your child know how important it is that she'll be doing something on her own and meeting new friends.

If there is an older sibling or if you know someone whose child attends the preschool your child will be attending, visit the place with your child often.

"Playing preschool" is another good way to prepare your child for the routine of school. If your child will ride a bus to school, you can pretend to ride a bus together.

Always be positive when talking about new experiences awaiting them in preschool. Stress fun and play and the variety of activities they will get a chance to do. Keep it positive—don't say things in a negative framework, such as "I'll bet you won't be scared about going to school alone at all." Odds are, if you don't introduce a negative possibility, it might never occur to your child.

It's the rare child who isn't at least a little anxious about starting preschool. Resist the temptation to say reassuring but exaggerated things such as "Preschool will be the most fun you've ever had!" Disney World is probably the most fun he's ever had—it's unlikely preschool will match that experience.

If your child seems afraid, never belittle those fears. Preschool may not seem like a big deal to you, but it most certainly is to a young child who doesn't have the advantage of your years of experience. Don't say "Don't be silly! It's just preschool. Everyone goes." If your child is afraid for whatever reason, it's definitely not "silly" to him.

Instead, help calm his fears by giving him information. Tell him what to expect when he gets to school—where he'll be going, what he'll be doing, and who will be in class with him.

Although you need to acknowledge the important step your child is taking, too much emphasis on the change may heighten her anxiety. Preschoolers can pick up on their parents' nonverbal cues. If you feel guilty or worried about leaving her at school, your child will probably sense that. The more calm and assured you are about your choice to send your child to preschool, the more confident your child will be.

Before School Begins ...

After you enroll your child in preschool but before the first day of class, it's a good idea to take your child along to visit the classroom a few times. While you're there, let your child explore and observe the class, deciding whether to interact with other children. The idea is to familiarize the child with the classroom and to let her get comfortable.

This is a good time to ask your child's future teacher what special procedures the school has for dealing with the first few days, when separation anxiety may make good-bye a tearful time.

If you suspect your child will find the new experience of separating during preschool painful, plan to spend some time with her in the class during the first few days. Ask the teacher to help you decide when it is right to reduce the time, and find out how the teacher plans to structure the first week to ensure a smooth transition for your child.

In the Next Chapter

Now that you've learned how to get your child ready for preschool, in the final chapter we'll discuss how to handle any problems once you get there.

Chapter 11

Preschool: You've Arrived!

At last, the big day has come. You've carefully researched all your options, interviewed the teachers and administrators, talked to other parents, and spent hours visiting the classroom to evaluate the program. The first day doesn't have to be traumatic for either of you. In this chapter, you'll discover some tips for making that first day a successful one.

The First Day

If you're starting a job or going back to work when your child enters her program, explain what you'll be doing while she's there. It may help her to think about you embarking on a new adventure, too.

Following are some tips to keep in mind for when you drop your child off at preschool that first day.

Don't Arrive Early

Avoid getting to school too early—it will only prolong the act of separation.

Reintroduce the Teacher

When you enter the classroom on the first day, calmly reintroduce the teacher to your child, then step back and let the teacher take control.

Your child's teacher will set the tone as she begins to form a relationship with your child. Your endorsement of the teacher will show your child that you trust the teacher to keep her happy and safe.

If your child clings to you or refuses to participate in the class, don't get upset. Follow the guidelines as described by the teacher beforehand.

Remember that even if a child is enthusiastic about preschool, he or she may still experience some fear when actually left with the teacher the first week.

Say Good-Bye

Never linger when it's time to say good-bye.

If she cries, screams, or clings to you, be supportive ("I know this is a little scary") but firm and calm. A long, sad farewell scene might only serve to reinforce a child's sense that preschool is a bad place.

Don't Sneak Out

Although you might be tempted to sneak out the back door when you drop off your child, don't. This will only cause more distress when your child realizes you're gone. As tempting as it may be, leaving without saying good-bye to your child—even if she's having a great time—risks her trust in you.

Spend a couple minutes with your child in the classroom, but when it's time to leave, say good-bye cheerfully. Give a quick kiss and hug if you think this won't embarrass your child, or call out a cheerful "See you after your song fest."

When the hugs are over, make sure your child is involved in some kind of activity before going. Don't drag it out or let on that you might be upset—just handle the leave-taking matter-of-factly and confidently, and your child will learn to do the same.

Once you've left, don't come back until it's time for your child to go home.

As hard as it may be, don't remove your child from the classroom if he cries, because bringing him home if he cries may reinforce the crying—and may even increase the crying throughout the adjustment period.

Don't Tease

It's even more important to resist the temptation to threaten or tease a child about being a "cry baby." Rarely does such a strategy help. Although it's only natural to become upset at separations, too many parents get angry in the face of their helplessness at their child's tears. Almost always, anger will only make things worse.

Instead, reassure your child that it's all right to cry when you miss someone you love. Remind her that you'll be reunited every afternoon and that as she makes new friends and gets used to things, she won't miss you so much.

If you're the one on the verge of tears as your child goes off to preschool for the first time, choke them back until she's well out of sight.

Don't ask your child tremulously "Will you be okay?" Instead, reassure her "I know you'll do fine." Accept your child's feelings without dwelling on them, and let her know that you understand that it takes time to get used to new people and places.

Think about your child's separation sensitivity, and recognize that different ages may react differently to separation. Many preschoolers age three and above want to establish themselves as separate from their parents and are more independent than children aged two years old and younger. Still, all preschoolers may be a bit nervous on the first day of school.

Parting Ritual

It's often helpful to develop a brief good-bye ritual—waving through the window or blowing a kiss from the doorway—so your child knows what to expect and you're not swayed to drag it out. Such a ritual can ease the separation.

You might say something like, "I'll be back to get you soon, long before we see the moon." Repeat this each time you drop off your child.

Coming up with an effective parting ritual was helpful for Angela, a Texas mom of three, when her oldest daughter developed severe separation anxiety at drop-off time. The two worked out a special good-bye ritual: Each morning, Ann would work on one puzzle with her daughter; then the teacher would walk the child to the window and they would wave good-bye.

After a month, Ann's daughter said, "You don't have to do the puzzle with me anymore." Another few months later, Ann's daughter announced she wanted to go to the window alone to wave good-bye to her mother. By the end of the year, Ann was able to drop off her daughter and leave immediately with no tears or tantrums.

If the program has rules that limit bringing in favorite toys (all schools are okay with nap toys and blankets), suggest that she bring a photo of you or of the family pet, or let her choose something that reminds her of you— perhaps one of your scarves.

Ease into the Day

Regardless of whether your child shows signs of separation anxiety, make sure that a school staff member is ready to help your child with the transfer from your care to the classroom when you arrive in the morning. Some children may need to be introduced into the activities of other children in a special way, whereas others might want a cuddle and a story from the teacher after you go.

Many preschools begin with their own daily ritual because they recognize the comfort such consistency can bring. Many schools opt for "circle time" first thing, when teachers and children can talk about what they did the day before and today's activities. This helps ease the transition from home to school.

Generally, young children will become more confident in their new environment and settle into a routine as time passes, but don't be surprised to find an occasional relapse into anxiety when you leave. Sometimes, a few months into the year, a child who has been enjoying preschool will suddenly stand at the window and cry when you go. Don't assume this means there's a sudden maladjustment; it might mean that your child is having a bad day. Children go through phases, just like grown-ups.

If your child's anxiety doesn't fade away after a few days, try to find out if there's a specific problem. Perhaps he's having trouble getting along with one other child in the group, or perhaps your child has misunderstood a rule and is worried about it. If you suspect that your child is not treated properly by the teacher or other staff, contact the school's director.

If your child is having a bad day, you may find it reassuring to call the preschool to check on how things are going. Don't be afraid to call the teacher later to ask whether your child has calmed down. You'll probably hear that your child stopped crying the minute you drove away.

Still, even if the transition was difficult with one child, it doesn't mean you'll have the same problems with a younger sibling. Both parents and youngsters need time to adapt, establish a routine, and adjust to this new and exciting experience.

At the End of the Day

If this is the first time your child will be away from you, she may worry that you're not coming back, or that you'll get lost and won't be able to find your way back to the school to pick her up at the end of the day. Or maybe you'll just forget to come! These are real fears for children this age.

Make sure your child understands that you know how to get to the school from wherever you'll be and that you know how to call the teachers, too. You may also want to mention that the grown-ups in charge will be able to call you if it's ever necessary. Stress the fact that there will always be someone there to take care of her.

Be clear about who will pick her up and when. Find out from the teacher what the last event of the day will be, and tell your child that she'll see you after the group does this activity.

Try to arrive a little early to pick up your child during the first week or so, to allow for a gradual adjustment to new schedules, routines, and the length of the stay. From then on, try very hard to ensure you're never late. Two minutes of waiting can seem excruciating to a child when "all the other kids" are gleefully greeting their parents.

Ask yourself how you can arrange your schedule so you can talk to the teacher every day, ask your child every day how the day went, and observe your child in preschool at different times of the day.

The Next Few Days

During the first few days, allow extra time to get your child ready and out the door in the morning, because the calmer life is at home, the easier the separation will be at preschool.

Allow some time for the transition. Your child may need you during the first few days starting the preschool, so it might be a good idea to take some time off work if you can. Expect to spend about an hour at the preschool during the first day with your child.

Each day, take a few minutes to talk about what happened at preschool. Prepare your child for extended holiday breaks ahead of time, because the sudden break in routine may upset your child. Point out the last week of school before winter or summer break.

Don't be worried if your best friend's daughter makes a faster adjustment to preschool than your child. No two children are the same. They are probably different in all of their daily activities. Some children have personalities that simply require them to spend a little more time settling in.

Realize that children react differently to transitions. Just because her cousin thrived at preschool from the very first day doesn't mean your child's adjustment will be the same. Read the signs carefully and get ready to provide reassurance and extra love and attention at home. Work with your child's teachers. They will tell you how the day went and how your child is adjusting.

If Your Child Has Trouble Adjusting

Talk to the teachers if you still have concerns about your child's adjustment after the first few weeks. With their experience watching many young children adjust to school, teachers are in the best position to let you know if your concerns are well founded.

If you have any doubts about the program, stop by unannounced. It's important to keep paying attention to what's going on and to make sure the preschool lives up to your expectations, too.

Your child's feelings about preschool are also important. Does she enjoy going to school, or is each day a battle? You also can get a good idea if your child is adjusting at school by talking to her. As you drive home, try asking your child what was fun or special about the day or which children she likes playing with. Many parents have found that all kinds of problems tumble out when the parent is in the front seat and the child is in the back; the lack of face-to-face contact seems to make sharing problems more comfortable. If your child hints that she doesn't like something or someone, encourage her to tell you about it.

If it's hard to get much information out of your child, don't poke and probe. Just make sure she knows you're willing to talk about anything.

Take every opportunity to visit the school and chat with the teachers. Ask their opinion about how your child is getting along, and show that you're open to suggestions on how you might help your child have the best possible experience.

When your child is adjusting to preschool, it's important to remember that whatever problems crop up are probably fairly normal. Be patient.

In the beginning, some children cry at every parting. Ask the teacher whether your child seems to be enjoying herself the rest of the time. If she is, you can be confident it's just a temporary separation problem. However, if she seems miserable for the entire preschool day, you may want to consider withdrawing your child and trying again when she's a bit older.

Don't criticize the teachers or the program in front of your child. If he hears you complaining about the illness rules or saying that his teacher is too inexperienced, your child may feel uncomfortable and resist settling in. It's important that your child believe you approve of the preschool and trust the teachers and staff where he spends his day.

The preschool years are a time of developing social skills, but not all children find making friends easy and natural. If your child seems to be having trouble making friends, suggest that he invite other children in the school over for a play date on a weekend. This will give you a good idea of what the problem might be.

Does he play well with the other children, or does he show off, boss them around, or try too hard? You may want to believe your child is perfect, but being realistic about his behavior will enable you to guide him gently toward developing better social skills.

It's also important to have your child attend the program on a regular basis. If you let her skip class one day because she begged for a day at home, or because she stayed up too late the night before, she'll probably start to fuss any time she'd prefer to stay at home.

Most children actually find preschool adjustment more difficult if they believe they have some choice over whether or not they attend each day. Make it clear that you expect your child to go to preschool unless she's sick.

Making Preschool Work

Just because you've found the perfect preschool doesn't mean your job is over. If you're expecting a lot from your child's teacher, the least you can do is try to be a model parent, too.

Be Prompt

Pick up your child on time. Teachers understand that emergencies do happen and you're bound to be late once in a while, but really try to be prompt. If you anticipate a delay early in the day, call the school.

Remember that your child's teacher has a life outside of school, too, and when you're late, you may make the teacher late for her own appointments she's scheduled for after hours. Teachers may have children of their own who must also be picked up on time.

It's important to let the staff know if your child's routine will change. If Aunt Barbara is in town and wants to pick up your child from preschool, you must tell the school. Staffers are not allowed to release your child to anyone but you, unless you give permission. If you'll be picking up your child early for a doctor's appointment, warn the preschool about that, too.

Fill Out Paperwork

Even before your child attends the first day of school you'll need to submit a range of documents such as immunization records and medical health release forms. State law mandates that all preschools comply with this law, so help your school out and hand in forms on time.

During the school year you'll need to sign permission slips for field trips or authorization for teachers to give your child medications, such as antibiotics for an infection. Sign these right away and turn them in.

Read all notices and mail you get from the school. If you see a sheaf of papers in your child's cubby, don't toss it in the trash—you might miss out on valuable information about upcoming activities that require your child to bring in something from home. Or there might be notices about school closings, field trips, or special events. Newsletters from school are not junk mail.

Keep Communication Open

While you're at it, check the bulletin board at the school for other announcements. If there are any upcoming meetings, be sure to attend. If you're unavailable because of your job or an emergency, let the staff know.

Whether it's a parent-teacher conference or a special workshop on temper tantrums, your school recommends these events because the staff truly feels they'll help you. And these events are a great way to meet other parents who'll gladly trade discipline stories and schedule play dates.

Talk regularly with your child's teachers and the school's director so you can find out what's expected of you. Be sure to read all the newsletters so you know what is happening each day. Let the teacher know you want to help her make preschool a good experience for your child.

Be Prepared

Make sure your child has all necessary supplies. A change of clothes stashed in her cubby is a good idea in case of spills and toilet accidents. If your child comes home wearing the spare clothing, make sure you bring a fresh set the next day.

If your teacher tells you your child's class is doing a special art project featuring pine cones or autumn leaves, be sure to send in whatever is requested. If your child is going to be turning milkweed pods into parrots and you happen to live in an area with lots of milkweed pods, it's a nice gesture to send in a few extra for those children who will inevitably forget. Extras are also appreciated by the teacher in case an item is damaged or destroyed during the project.

Volunteer!

If the school has opportunities for parents to get involved, such as going on trips or helping with activities, be the first to sign up. You'll not only help the school, you'll get a chance to better understand what your child does all day—and your child will love the chance to show you off.

Don't Pass Germs Around

Children in preschool are more likely to get sick because they're around more children. To help decrease the chance of passing on colds and other viruses, children with contagious illnesses should stay home. Report any illnesses to your center or preschool. Children share germs quite easily, so your teacher needs to know if your child has been exposed to any highly contagious diseases such as pinkeye or chicken pox, or to critters like lice.

Fever, irritability, lethargy, persistent crying, or difficulty breathing can all be signs of illness.

In practice, this tends to get more complicated than it sounds. By the time some diseases are diagnosed, a child may no longer be contagious and can usually return to school right away.

Your preschool will probably have specific rules about illness, but in general a child shouldn't go to preschool if he has any of the following:

- Upper respiratory illness: Bronchitis or influenza will likely make your child feel quite sick; youngsters should not return to school until fever is normal and other symptoms have passed.

- Fever: A child with a fever should definitely stay home and come back to school after being fever free for 24 hours.

- Gastrointestinal illness: A child with diarrhea that can't be contained by diapers or by using the toilet regularly should stay home until the condition improves. Children whose stools are bloody or filled with mucus should stay home, because this could be the sign of a viral or bacterial infection.

- Vomiting: A child who is vomiting or who has vomited in the night should skip preschool the next day.

- Rash: If you're sure it's linked to an infection (many aren't), your child should stay home; if your child's rash is not linked to a fever or other symptoms, it's probably okay to go to preschool. A rash associated with an illness rather than dry skin or eczema has usually stopped being contagious by the time the rash appears (see chicken pox). A rash following a measles, mumps, or rubella (MMR) vaccination is not contagious.

- Chicken pox: Children with chicken pox can return to school on the sixth day after their rash appears, or sooner if the sores have dried and crusted over.

- Impetigo: Children with this contagious skin disease can go back to preschool after 24 hours of antibiotics.

- Scabies: Children with this infestation can return to school after treatment.

- Bacterial conjunctivitis (pinkeye): A child can go back to preschool after 24 hours of antibiotics. A child with nonbacterial conjunctivitis with red eyes and clear, watery discharge doesn't need antibiotics and can return to school immediately.

- Strep throat: A child can go back to school after 24 hours of antibiotics.
- Mouth sores: Wait until your child's doctor says he's not infectious before he returns to school.
- Head lice: Your child can return to school after being thoroughly treated.

Let teachers know if your child needs extra care for some reason. Perhaps your child didn't sleep well last night or your spouse is away on a business trip. Perhaps a family pet has died or a relative is ill. If you let the teacher know, she'll be able to give your child some extra attention.

The Best Choice

No school will be perfect for every child all the time. Joining in a group means that sometimes your child will have to adapt to the needs of the group.

One of the main reasons for spending so much time choosing a good preschool is that it's easier to help your child through the adjustment period if you're sure the preschool is a healthy and sensitive one. Such confidence will make it easier for you to reassure her that she will be all right.

By trusting your instincts and keeping your eyes open, you can find the one preschool that is comfortable for your child most of time.

Appendix A

Preschool-Related Organizations

Association for Childhood Education International
17904 Georgia Avenue, Suite 215
Olney, MD 20832
301-570-2111 or 1-800-423-3563
Fax: 301-570-2212
www.udel.edu/bateman/acei/

Association of Waldorf Schools of North America
3911 Bannister Road
Fair Oaks, CA 95628
916-961-0927
www.awsna.org

Child Care Action Campaign
330 Seventh Avenue, 17th Floor
New York, NY 10001
212-239-0138

Child Care Aware
1-800-424-2246

Childtime Learning Centers
38345 West 10 Mile Road, Suite 100
Farmington Hills, MI 48335
866-CHILDTIME (866-244-5384)
www.childtime.com

The Early Childhood Education Organization
Linden Park Junior Primary School
14 Hay Road
Linden Park, SA 5065
www.echo.asn.au/content.htm

ERIC Clearinghouse on Elementary and Early Childhood Education
University of Illinois
805 West Pennsylvania Avenue
Urbana, IL 61801
217-333-1386 or 1-800-583-4135
ericps.ed.uiuc.edu/ericeece.html

I Am Your Child
1325 6th Avenue, 30th Floor
New York, NY 10019
212-636-5030
Fax: 212-636-5868
Or:
PO Box 15605
Beverly Hills, CA 90209
310-285-2385
Fax: 310-205-2760
www.iamyourchild.org

National Association of Child Care Resources and Referral Agencies
2116 Campus Drive SE
Rochester, MN 55904
507-287-2020

National Association for the Education of Young Children
1509 16th Street, NW
Washington, DC 20036-1426
202-232-8777 or 1-800-424-2460
Fax: 202-328-1846
www.naeyc.org

National Association of State Boards of Education
1012 Cameron Street
Alexandria, VA 22314
703-684-4000

National Coalition for Early Childhood Professionals
PO Box 358
Lynnfield, MA 01940
617-284-6092 or 508-255-4350

National Head Start Association
1651 Prince Street
Alexandria, VA 22314
703-739-0875
www.nhsa.org

National PTA
330 N. Wabash Avenue, Suite 2100
Chicago, IL 60611
312-951-6782

National Resource Center for Health and Safety in Child Care
1-800-598-KIDS (1-800-598-5437)

University of Illinois Children's Research Center
51 Gerty Drive
Champaign, IL 61820-7469
217-333-1386 or 1-800-583-4135
Fax: 217-333-3767
ericeece.org

Websites Only

The ABCs of Safe and Healthy Child Care
www.cdc.gov/ncidod/hip/ABC/abc.htm

Child Care Aware
www.childcareaware.org

Early Education Clearinghouse—Facts in Act
www.factsinaction.org

National Child Care Information Center (NCCIC)
nccic.org/

National Early Childhood Technical Assistance Program
www.nectas.unc.edu

National Institute on Early Childhood Development and Education
www.ed.gov/offices/oeri/eci

National Network for Child Care
www.nncc.org

National Resource Center for Health and Safety in Child Care
www.nrc.uchsc.edu

Special Education, Learning Disabilities
www.iser.com/index.shtml

Special Education, Learning Disabilities Advocacy, Legal Advice
www.iser.com/Cadvocacy.html

U.S. National Committee of the World Organization for Early Childhood Education
omep-usnc.org

Appendix B

Phone Prescreening Checklist

Use the following printable checklist to jot down notes when calling centers.

School name: _____

Address: _____

Phone number: _____

Director: _____

Business hours: _____

Cost weekly: _____

Cost daily: _____

- ❑ Is there an opening for my child?
- ❑ What hours and days are you open?
- ❑ Is preenrollment required?
- ❑ What are the eligibility requirements?
- ❑ What is the school's educational philosophy?

- ❑ Can you describe a typical day's activities?
- ❑ Do you teach letters and numbers?
- ❑ How much does care cost? Is financial assistance available?
- ❑ How many children are in your care?
- ❑ What age groups do you serve?
- ❑ Do you provide transportation?
- ❑ Do you provide meals (breakfast, lunch, dinner, snacks)?
- ❑ How are absences and vacations handled?
- ❑ What is the policy on withdrawals and dismissal?
- ❑ Do you have a license, accreditation, or other certification?
- ❑ Do you encourage drop-in visits?
- ❑ May I have a list of references?

Appendix C

First Visit Checklist

The following checklist is based on criteria furnished by the National Association for the Education of Young Children (NAEYC).

The First Visit

- ❑ Were you greeted warmly by the teacher and/or administrator?
- ❑ Is there a parent bulletin board to let you know what's happening in the school?
- ❑ Is the preschool registered with the state?
- ❑ Is there space for your child?
- ❑ If not, can you get on a waiting list?
- ❑ Are pick-up and drop-off times flexible?
- ❑ Is there a "late pick-up" fee?
- ❑ Do teachers encourage visits from parents at any time?

Staff

- ❑ Are the teachers certified?
- ❑ Are teachers specially trained for the age they teach?

- ❑ Do they have diplomas in early childhood education?
- ❑ Does the staff have up-to-date first-aid certificates?
- ❑ Did the teacher give you at least three professional references?
- ❑ Did you feel comfortable asking questions?
- ❑ Did the director offer more information?
- ❑ Does the school have a parent board or parents' committee?
- ❑ Are teachers interacting pleasantly with the children?
- ❑ Are the teachers warm and friendly?
- ❑ Do teachers supervise sufficiently when children are socializing?
- ❑ Do teachers interact with children in both small and large group activities?

Environment

- ❑ Was the indoor temperature adequate?
- ❑ Was the room stuffy?
- ❑ Does the school smell clean inside?
- ❑ Is the room well lit?
- ❑ While you're at work, will you feel comfortable knowing your child is in this setting?

Safety Issues

- ❑ Are the toys washed on a regular basis?
- ❑ Are the bathrooms clean?
- ❑ Are there gates in front of the stairways?
- ❑ Are outlets covered?
- ❑ Is there a fenced and monitored playground with outdoor toys and climbing structures?
- ❑ Are the teachers and director trained in CPR?
- ❑ Was there a first-aid kit in a prominent location?
- ❑ Did you see fire extinguishers and posted fire escape plans?

Health Issues

❑ Are the lunches and snacks prepared onsite?

❑ Are breakfast, lunch, and two snacks provided daily?

❑ Is the menu posted?

❑ Does the menu include meat, fruits, vegetables, and dairy?

❑ Does the school provide only fried food and junk food?

❑ How does the school handle children with food allergies?

❑ Can the director give medication to your child?

❑ What is the policy on infectious diseases?

❑ Are immunizations required?

❑ Is there a snack in the morning and one in the afternoon?

❑ Do teachers wash their hands frequently?

Activities

❑ Are there weekly "themes" such as seasons and holidays?

❑ Are running, jumping, dancing, and moving encouraged?

❑ Are drawing, cutting, painting, and gluing encouraged?

❑ Did you see puzzles, books, games, and lots of toys?

❑ Are there puppets and dolls?

❑ Is there a written, planned program you can see in action?

❑ Is the curriculum adapted for children at different levels of development?

❑ Was the classroom divided into centers?

❑ Is talking and singing encouraged?

❑ Do children go outside every day (weather permitting)?

❑ Did the children seem relaxed and happy?

❑ How many children were there per teacher?

❑ Is there a policy for vacations and holidays?

❑ If a child doesn't want to participate, is his decision respected?

❑ Do children have access to a variety of engaging activities throughout the day?

❑ Are children read to throughout the day?

❑ Do children have ample time to play and explore?

Appendix D

Parents: Read More About It

Anti-Bias Curriculum: Tools for Empowering Young Children by Louise Derman-Sparks

Caring Spaces, Learning Places: Children's Environments That Work by Jim Greenman

Child Development/Parenting Child Behavior: The Classic Childcare Manual from the Gesell Institute of Human Development by Frances L. Ilg and Louise B. Ames

Creative Expression and Play in Early Childhood by Joan Packer Isenberg and Mary Renck Jalongo

Creative Resources for Infants and Toddlers by Judy Herr and Terri Swim

Developmentally Appropriate Practice in Early Childhood Programs by Sue Bredekamp and Carol Copple

Don't Move the Muffin Tins: A Hands-Off Guide to Art for the Young Child by Bev Bos

First Feelings: Milestones in the Emotional Development of Your Baby and Child by Stanley I. Greenspan, M.D.

From Neurons to Neighborhoods: The Science of Early Childhood Development by Jack P. Shonkoff, ed., et al

Mudpies to Magnets by Robert E. Rockwell, Elizabeth A. Sherwood, and Robert A. Williams

Open the Door, Let's Explore More by Rhoda Redleaf

Play in the Lives of Children by Cosby Rogers and Janet Sawyers

Please Don't Sit on the Kids by Clare Cherry

School-Age Ideas and Activities for After School Programs by Karen Haas-Foletta and Michele Cogley

So This Is Normal Too? by Deborah Hewitt

Squish, Sort, Paint, and Build: Over 200 Easy Learning Center Activities by Sharon MacDonald

Story Stretchers: Activities to Expand Children's Favorite Books by Shirley C. Raines, Kathleen Charner, ed., with Robert J. Canady

Teaching in the Key of Life by Mimi Chenfeld

Theories of Childhood: An Introduction to Dewey, Montessori, Erickson, Piaget and Vygotsky by Carol Garhart Mooney

Touchpoints by T. Berry Brazelton

Appendix E

Good Preschool Picture Books

Reading to your child is a great way to prepare her for preschool. The following list includes a variety of excellent choices of preschool picture books recommended for both classroom teachers and parents. Preschool books are listed according to early childhood education themes.

Animal Books

Adam Mouse's Book of Poems by Lilian Moore

Animal Babies by Arthur Gregor

Animals Should Definitely Not Wear Clothing by Judi and Ron Barrett

Beastly Banquet: Tasty Treats for Animal Appetites: Animal Poems by Peggy Munsterberg

Big Red Barn by Margaret Wise Brown, illustrated by Felicia Bond

Boo to a Goose by Mem Fox, illustrated by David Miller

Cluck by Alan Snow

Dibble and Dabble by Dave and Julie Saunders

Dinosaur! by Peter Sis

Dinosaurs Forever by William Wise, illustrated by Lynn Munsinger

Dr. Duck by H. M. Ehrlich, illustrated by Laura Rader

Five Little Kittens by Nancy Jewell, illustrated by Elizabeth Sayles

Four Fur Feet by Margaret Wise Brown

If You Give a Moose a Muffin by Laura Numeroff

If You Give a Mouse a Cookie by Laura Numeroff

If You Give a Pig a Pancake by Laura Numeroff

Is Your Mama a Llama? by Deborah Guarino, illustrated by Steven Kellogg

Jafta by Hugh Lewin, illustrated by Lisa Kopper

Mr. Gumpy's Outing by John Burningham

Owl Babies by Martin Waddell, illustrated by Patrick Benson

Patrick's Dinosaurs by Carol Carrick, illustrated by Donald Carrick

Rosie's Walk by Pat Hutchins

Seven Little Rabbits by John Becker

Spot's First Walk by Eric Hill

Tabby: A Story in Pictures by Aliki Brandenberg

Ten Flashing Fireflies, Philemon Sturges

Who Is Tapping at My Window? by A. G. Deming, illustrated by Monica Wellington

Alphabet Books

26 Letters and 99 Cents by Tana Hoban

A B C by Karen Gundersheimer

"A" for Antarctica by Jonathan Chester

Albert's Alphabet by Leslie Tryon

Alphabatics by Sue McDonald

Alphabet Apartments by Lesley Moyes

Arlene Alda's A, B, C by Arlene Alda

Beach Ball by Peter Sis

Eating the Alphabet by Lois Ehlert

Farm Alphabet by Jane Miller

First Steps by John Burningham

Halloween ABC by Eve Merriam, illustrated by Lane Smith

Colors, Shapes, and Counting

Afro-Bets: Books of Colors by Margery W. Brown, illustrated by Culverson Blair

Brown Bear, Brown Bear, What Do You See? by Bill Martin Jr., illustrated by Eric Carle

Colors by Lois Ehlert

Go Away, Big Green Monster! by Ed Emberley

Green Eggs and Ham by Dr. Seuss

Harold and the Purple Crayon by Crockett Johnson

Is It Red? Is It Yellow? Is It Blue? by Tana Hoban

It Looked Like Spilt Milk by Charles G. Shaw

Little Blue and Little Yellow by Leo Lionni

Mary Wore Her Red Dress and Henry Wore His Green Sneakers, adapted and illustrated by Merle Peek

Mr. Rabbit and the Lovely Present by Charlotte Zolotow, illustrated by Maurice Sendak

Of Colors and Things by Tana Hoban

Planting a Rainbow by Lois Ehlert

A Rainbow of My Own by Don Freeman

Red Is Best by Kathy Stinson, illustrated by Robin Baird Lewis

Round and Round and Round by Tana Hoban

Shapes by Karen Gundersheimer

Shapes by Keith Faulkner, illustrated by Jonathan Lambert

Shapes, Shapes, Shapes by Tana Hoban

So Many Circles, So Many Squares by Tana Hoban

What a Wonderful World by George David Weiss and Bob Thiele

The Very Hungry Caterpillar by Eric Carle

Self-Concept

Alexander and the Terrible, Horrible, No Good, Very Bad Day by Judith Viorst, illustrated by Ray Cruz

Ask Mr. Bear by Marjorie Flack

Being Bullied by Kate Petty, illustrated by Charlotte Firmin

Chrysanthemum by Kevin Henkes

Corduroy by Don Freeman

Crow Boy by Taro Yashima

Exploring Feelings by Susan B. Neuman and Renee P. Panoff

The Grouchy Ladybug by Eric Carle

Hands Are Not for Hitting by Martine Agassi, illustrated by Marieka Heinlen

I Love You Forever by Robert Munsch, illustrated by Sheila McGraw

I Wish I Was Sick, Too! by Franz Brandenberg, illustrated by Aliki

Ira Sleeps Over by Bernard Waber

It's Mine! by Leo Lionni

Jess Was the Brave One by Jean Little

Making Faces by Nick Butterworth

Mama Cat Has Three Kittens by Denise Fleming

The Meanest Thing to Say by Bill Cosby

My Mama Says There Aren't Any Zombies, Ghosts, Vampires, Creatures, Demons, Monsters, Fiends, Goblins, or Things by Judith Viorst, illustrated by Kay Chorao

No Matter What by Debi Gliori

No, David! by David Shannon

Oliver Button Is a Sissy by Tomie dePaola

Olivia by Ian Falconer

On the Day You Were Born by Debra Frasier

Pete's Pizza by William Steig

Peter's Chair by Ezra Jack Keats

The Pig in a Wig by Alan MacDonald, illustrated by Paul Hess

Rosie's Story by Martine Gogoll

Sad Monster, Glad Monster by Ed Emberly

Sam by Herbert Scott, illustrated by Symeon Shimin

The Snowy Day by Ezra Jack Keats

Some Things Are Different, Some Things Are the Same by Marya Dantzer-Rosenthal, illustrated by Miriam Nerlove

Sometimes I Like to Curl Up in a Ball by Vicki Churchill, illustrated by Charles Fudge

Swimmy by Leo Lionni

Toot & Puddle by Holly Hobbie

Where Can It Be? by Ann Jonas

Where the Wild Things Are by Maurice Sendak

William's Doll by Charlotte Zolotow, illustrated by William Pene duBois

You Smell and Taste and Feel and See and Hear by Mary Murphy

Your Belly Button by Jun Nanao, illustrated by Tomoko Hasegava

Social Development

Alfie Gives a Hand by Shirley Hughes

All Fall Down by Helen Oxenbury

Best Friends by Miriam Cohen, illustrated by Lillian Hoban

Cherries and Cherry Pits by Vera B. Williams

A Friend Is Someone Who Likes You by Joan Walsh Anglund

Friends by Helme Heine

Friends by Rachel Isadora

George and Martha One Fine Day by James Marshall

The Giving Tree by Shel Silverstein

If You Give a Moose a Muffin by Laura Joffe Numeroff, illustrated by Felicia Bond

If You Give a Mouse a Cookie by Laura Joffe Numeroff, illustrated by Felicia Bond

If You Give a Pig a Pancake by Laura Joffe Numeroff, illustrated by Felicia Bond

May I Bring a Friend? by Beatrice Schenk DeRegniers, illustrated by Beni Montresor

Messy Bessey's Closet by Patricia and Fredrick McKissack, illustrated by Ricky Hackney

Mirandy and Brother Wind by Patricia C. McKissack, illustrated by Jerry Pinkney

One for You and One for Me by Wendy Blaxland, illustrated by Janice Bowles

The Rain Came Down by David Shannon

The Rainbow Fish by Marcus Pfister

Rose and Dorothy by Roslyn Schwartz

The Selfish Crocodile by Charles Faustin, illustrated by Michael Terry

Stone Soup by Marcia Brown

What If the Zebras Lost Their Stripes? by John Reitano, illustrated by William Haines

Will I Have a Friend? by Miriam Cohen, illustrated by Lillian Hoban

Willie's Not the Hugging Kind by Joyce Durham Barrett, illustrated by Pat Cummings

Farm Books

Baby Farm Animals by Garth Williams

Barn by Debby Atwell

Barnyard Dance by Sandra Boynton

Barnyard Lullaby by Frank Asch

Big Red Barn by Margaret Wise Brown

Bunny Reads Back: Old MacDonald by Rosemary Wells

Cock-a-Doodle-Moo by Bernard Most

Count the Farm Animals 1-2-3 by Rosalinda Kightley

The Day the Sheep Showed Up by David M. McPhail

Dora's Eggs by Julie Sykes, illustrated by Jane Chapman

Egg Poems by John Foster

Farm Alphabet Book by Jane Miller

Farmer Mack Measures His Pig by Tony Johnston

Hamm the Tiny, Tiny Boy and the Big, Big Cow by Nancy VanLaan, illustrated by Margorie Priceman

Once in the Country: Poems of a Farm by Tony Johnston

Over on the Farm: A Counting Picture Book Rhyme by Christopher Gunson

Rock-a-Bye Farm by Diane Johnston

Food

At the Supermarket by David Hautzig

Banana Moon by Janet Marshall

Don't Forget the Bacon! by Pat Hutchins

Do the Doors Open by Magic? And Other Supermarket Questions by Catherine Ripley

Doodle Soup: Poems by John Ciardi

Eating the Alphabet: Fruits and Vegetables from A to Z by Lois Ehlert

Feast for Ten by Cathryn Falwell

In the Supermarket by Henry Pluckrose

My Shopping List by Samantha Berger, illustrated by Michael Reid

One Lonely Sea Horse, Saxton Frymann and Joost Elffers

Pickin' Peas by Margaret R. McDonald, illustrated by Pat Cummings

Sweets & Treats: Dessert Poems by Bobbye Goldstein

Tasty Poems by Jill Bennett

To Market, to Market by Anne Miranda, illustrated by Janet Stevens

Tommy at the Grocery Store by Bill Grossman

Where Are You? by Francesca Simon and David Melling

Multicultural Books

A Is for Africa by Ifeoma Onyefulu

Abuela's Weave by Omar S. Castaneda

Amelia's Road by Linda Jacobs

Altman Anansi the Spider: A Tale from the Ashanti by Gerald McDermott

At the Beach by Huy Voun Lee

Buenas Noches, Luna by Margeret Wise Brown

Come with Me to Africa: A Photographic Journey by Gregory Scott

The Day of Ahmed's Secret by Florence Parry Heide and Judith Heide Gilliland

Everybody Bakes Bread by Norah Dooley

Everybody Cooks Rice by Norah Dooley

Fire Race: A Karuk Coyote Tale About How Fire Came to the People, retold by Jonathan London with Lanny Pinola

Hanukkah by Alan Benjamin

How My Parents Learned to Eat by Ina R. Friedman

In My Mother's House by Ann Nolan Clark

Jaha and Jamil Went Down the Hill: An African Mother Goose by Birginia L. Kroll

Kente Colors by Debbi M. Chocolate, illustrated by John Ward

Kreikemeir Emeka's Gift: An African Counting Story by Ifeoma Onyefulu

Mama, Do You Love Me? by Barbara M. Joosse

The Man on the Flying Trapeze: The Circus Life of Emmett Kelly Sr. by Robert Quackenbush

Margaret and Margarita (bilingual English/Spanish) by Lynn Reiser

The Mitten: A Ukranian Folktale by Jan Brett

Mouse Match: A Chinese Folktale by Ed Young

New Shoes for Silva by Johnna Hurwitz, illustrated by Jerry Pickney

Noko and the Night Monster by Fiona Moodie

Not Yet Yvette by Helen Ketterman

Shake It to the One That You Love the Best: Plays, Songs and Lullabies from Black Musical Traditions, collected and adapted by Cheryl Warren Mattox

Shoes, Shoes, Shoes by Ann Morris Somos

Ten Oni Drummers by Mathew Gollub

Tikki Tikki Tembo, Blair Lent, illustrator, retold by Arlene Mosel

Too Many Tamales by Gary Soto

Un arco iris (We Are a Rainbow) by Nancy Maria Grande Tabor

The Village of Round and Square Houses by Ann Grifalconi

Welcoming Babies by Margy Burns Knight

Zomo the Rabbit: A Trickster Tale from West Africa by Gerald McDermott

Tall Tales, Funny Books, and Folk Tales

Abiyoyo, based on a South African lullaby and folk story, text by Pete Seeger, illustrated by Michael Hays

Bringing the Rain to Kapiti Plain by Verna Aardema, illustrated by Beatriz Vidal

Cloudy with a Chance of Meatballs by Judi Barret

Fire Race: A Karuk Coyote Tale, retold by Jonathan London, illustrated by Sylvia Long

The Giant Jam Sandwich by John Vernon Lord, verses by Janet Burroway

Gregory, the Terrible Eater by Mitchell Sharmat, illustrated by Jose Aruego and Ariane Dewy

How the Turtle Got His Shell, adapted by Sandra Robbins, illustrated by Iku Oseki

The Hunterman and the Crocodile: A West African Folktale by Baba Wague Diakite

The Knee-High Man, adapted by William Miller, illustrated by Roberta Glidden

Magic Pebble by William Steig

Mufaro's Beautiful Daughters by John Steptoe

The Paper Dragon by Marguerite W. Davol, illustrated by Robert Sabuda

Snow and the Sun/la Nieve y el Sol: A South American Folk Rhyme in Two Languages, translated by Antonio Frasconi Sylvester

Strega Nona by Tomie De Paola

The Talking Eggs by Robert San Souci

There Was an Old Lady Who Swallowed a Fly by Simms Taback

We're Going on a Bear Hunt by Michael J. Rosen, illustrated by Helen Oxenbury

Why Mosquitoes Buzz in People's Ears by Verna Aardema, illustrated by Leo and Diane Dillon

Appendix F

Infants in Child-Care Centers

A lot of working parents of infants don't have many child-care options. It's unfortunate that in most cases, parents work far from home and the nearest relatives live across the country. Added to this is the fact that for most people, family leave may be as short as several weeks, and even in the best cases doesn't usually exceed three months. What's a new family to do?

Baby-sitting might sound like an option, but often you'll find that your working hours might not coincide with theirs. On other hand, having a live-in nanny is usually expensive and requires lots of extra space in the house, which might be a little more costly than you can manage.

The conclusion many young parents make is to start looking for a good child-care center—and the earlier the better. Your best bet is to call your local referral agency to find out where to look, what options you have, and how much it will cost. Referral agencies will also provide you with useful tips, brochures, and other services.

By now you're probably familiar with the fact that learning starts from the very first days of life. You know that your child needs love and bonding with a trusting adult when you can't be around.

Good child-care centers develop their programs with the same concerns in mind. They make sure that their facilities and staff provide safe, nurturing, and stimulating care for the youngest ones.

Staff

The first thing you'll see in a good nursery program is the proper teacher-child ratio. Teachers should not have to take care of more than two or three infants at any given time and should have an assistant handy. Teachers must be able to respond quickly to children's needs. Infants develop different sleeping and feeding schedules, and individual attention at this age is crucial.

Infants need human touch and familiar faces. The staff should be warm, knowledgeable, and experienced. Teachers should hold babies and talk, sing, and read to them. They should be accepting of children's individualities, personality, bodies, and physical needs. Their attitudes should be positive and enthusiastic.

Teachers should also maintain careful records about individual children and respect parents' input. There should be good communication between teachers and parents, and the staff should readily accommodate your baby's special needs.

Of course, a high level of hygiene is a prerogative for all child-care staff. They should wash their hands before and after feeding, diapering, and whenever handling any body secretions. In some centers, teachers are given sanitary gloves to protect children and staff.

Daily disinfection of toys and changing, playing, and feeding areas is a must.

Older infants need even more individual attention. They explore their surroundings by touching, tasting, and manipulating objects and are curious about other children. Teachers should always be ready with positive instructions, encouragement in a reassuring voice, age-appropriate toys, and various teaching materials.

Environment

Don't get discouraged, because not all preschools were built for the purpose of accommodating infants. However, you'll find that many older buildings have been adapted quite well to serve young children.

Before opening infant rooms, preschools have to comply with many safety and sanitary regulations. Good infant rooms should be clean and bright, with separate activity, feeding, diapering, and sleeping areas. This ensures sanitation and helps contain the noise level.

Children should have their own cribs, bedding, feeding utensils, clothing, and diapers and should be allowed to have comforting objects brought from home. All personal objects should be labeled.

Activity areas should be carpeted, with lots of floor pillows and soft mats. Climbing and tumbling equipment should be padded. Colors in the room should be pleasant and bright (infants find color contrasts interesting).

Infants should be supervised at all times but not be confined to cribs and playpens. They should be able to move freely and be allowed to explore.

During the day, infants should spend time in different areas of the room and get used to various environments. Walls should be decorated with mirrors and pictures of human faces, friendly animals, and other familiar objects. Diversity should be presented in many forms.

Age-appropriate books should be sturdy with rounded edges. Toys should be made of different textures and stacked on low, open shelves in an inviting, colorful display. Children this young learn a lot by touching and are intrigued by different textures. Toys with small removable parts are not acceptable because of choking hazards.

Electrical outlets should be covered, and there should not be any exposed cords or hazardous materials. Floors are free of food scraps, dirt, and other small objects that might easily end up in a child's mouth.

Safety Tips

All child-care centers must comply with basic safety requirements and regulations. You should be aware that infant rooms should always be located on ground level and have wide enough doors for an easier evacuation of cribs and strollers.

Common sense will tell you that there might be times when you will need to get to your child fast. Be practical when choosing the center. Ask yourself how fast can you get to the center to pick your child up if necessary. Will you (or, in the worst case scenario, the ambulance) be stopped by gridlock? How far is the hospital? Does the staff have enough experience and ability to handle emergencies properly?

Infant teachers must have CPR and first-aid training. They must be coached and instructed in what to do in case of fire and other accidents; some centers have medical experts onsite. All emergency numbers, including the Poison Control Center, should be posted in highly visible locations.

If you decide to enroll your child in the center, you should be thoroughly informed about the school's emergency procedures and will probably be asked to sign a consent form or two.

References

American Montessori Society. *The American Montessori Society Profile.* January 2002. www.amshq.org.

The Association for Childhood Education International. *Standardized Tests for Young Children? Not Yet! A Position Paper on Standardized Testing.* Spring 1991, pp. 130–142. users.sgi.net/~cokids.

Blezard, Rob. *Operation Child Care.* Ford Foundation Report, Winter 2001. www.fordfound.org/publications.

Casper, Lynn. "Child Care Arrangements." U.S. Census Bureau, *Current Population Reports*, October, 1996. www.census.gov/population.

———. "What Does It Cost to Mind Our Preschoolers?" U.S. Census Bureau, *Current Population Reports*, September 1995, pp. 52–70. www.census.gov/population.

Galinsky, Ellen, and Dana E. Friedman. *Education Before School: Investing in Quality Child Care.* New York: Scholastic, Inc., 1993.

Gardener, Ralph. "A Kindergarten Crib Sheet." *New York Magazine.* New York, 1999.

Grace, Cathy. "The Portfolio and Its Use: Developmentally Appropriate Assessment of Young Children." Educational Resources Information Center, Clearinghouse on Elementary and Early Childhood Education, *ERIC/EECE Digest*, University of Illinois—Children's Research Center, 1992. ericeece.org.

Hale, Cynthia M., and Jacqueline A. Polder. *The ABCs of Safe and Healthy Child Care: An Online Handbook for Child Care Providers*, Department of Health and Human Services U.S. Public Health Services, Centers for Disease Control and Prevention, January 1997. www.cdc.gov/ncidod/hip/ABC.htm.

Leach, Penelope. *Children First: What Society Must Do—and Is Not Doing—for Children Today.* New York: Vintage Books—Random House, Inc., 1995.

Montessori, Maria. *The Absorbent Mind.* New York: Delta Books, Bantam Doubleday Dell Publishing Group, Inc., 1989.

National Association for the Education of Young Children. *Developmen-tally Appropriate Practice in Early Childhood Programs Serving Children from Birth Through Age Eight.* Washington, D.C., 1992. www.naeyc.org.

———. *NAEYC Early Childhood Program Accreditation: A Commitment to Excellence.* Position Statement, Washington, D.C., August 1996. www.naeyc.org.

———. *Position Statement Summary, Standardized Testing of Young Children 3 Through 8 Years of Age.* Washington, D.C., March 1998. www.naeyc. org/resources/position statements/pstestin.htm.

National Institute of Child Health and Human Development. *Children Score Higher on Tests When Child Care Meets Professional Standards,* News Release, July 1999. www.nichd.nih/gov/new/releases.

National Women's Law Center. *Child Care: Frequently Asked Questions, Federal and State Child Care Policy, Child Care Information, Copyright 2000.* www.nwlc.org/display.cfm?section=childcare.

New, Rebecca. "Reggio Emilia: Some Lessons for U.S. Educators." ED354988, *Eric Digests,* 1993. www.ed.gov/databases/ERIC-Digests.

New Jersey Inclusive Child Care Project of the Statewide Parent Advocacy Network (SPAN). *Child Care and Children with Special Needs.* New Jersey Inclusive Child Care Position Statement, Newark, NJ. www.spannj.org.

New Jersey State Department of Education, Division of Early Childhood Education. *Early Childhood Education Program Expectations: Standards of Quality,* April 2000.

Peth-Pierce, Robin. *The NICHD Study of Early Child Care,* National Institute of Child Health and Human Development-Public Information and Communications Branch, April 2000. www.nichd.nih.gov/publications.

Pope-Edwards, Carolyn, and Kay Wright-Springate. "Encouraging Creativity in Early Childhood Classroom." *ERIC/EECE Publications-Digests,* EDO-PS-9514, December 1995. ericeece.org.pubs/digests.

Stevens, G. Gwen, and Karen DeBord. "Issues of Assesment in Testing Children Under Age Eight." *The Forum,* North Carolina State University: Volume 6, No 2, Spring, 2001. www.ces.ncsu.edu/depts/fcs/pub/2001.

U.S. Centers for Disease Control (CDC), Division of Healthcare Quality Promotion (DHQP). *Issues in Child Care Settings.* January 1997. www.cdc.gov/ncidod/hip/abc/policie6.htm.

U.S. Department of Education, Office of Special Education Programs. *Office of Special Education Programs (OSEP) Mission.* June 2001. www.ed.gov/offices/OSERS/OSEP/About/aboutmission.html.

U.S. Department of Justice. *Commonly Asked Questions About Child Care Centers and the Americans with Disabilities Act.* October 1997. www.usdoj.gov/ada/childq&a.

U.S. Department of the Treasury. *Investing in Child Care: Challenges Facing Working Parents and the Private Sector Response.* Washington, D.C., 1999. www.treasury.gov.

Vedantam, Shankar. "Child Aggressiveness Cites Day Care." *Washington Post*, Washington, D.C., April 2001, p. A06.

Vobjeda, Barbara. "Who's Minding the Children?" *Washington Post*, Washington, D.C., October 1997, p. A01.

Wisconsin Education Association Council. Education Issues Series: *Special Education Inclusion*, November 2001. www.weac.org/resource.

Index

C

G–H